# ENCOUNTER
*of the*
# FAITHS

GEORGE WAYLAND CARPENTER

*FRIENDSHIP PRESS*   *New York*

LIBRARY OF CONGRESS CATALOG CARD NUMBER: 67-11852

# Contents

. . . What is faith? Faith gives substance to our hopes, and makes us certain of realities we do not see. . . .

By faith we perceive that the universe was fashioned by the word of God, so that the visible came forth from the invisible. . . .

It is for their faith that the men of old stand on record. . . .

They were not yet in possession of the things promised, but had seen them far ahead and hailed them. . . . That is why God is not ashamed to be called their God; for he has a city ready for them. (Hebrews 11:1, 3, 2, 13, 16, NEB)

And what of ourselves? With all these witnesses to faith around us like a cloud, we must throw off every encumbrance . . . and run with resolution the race for which we are entered, our eyes fixed on Jesus, on whom faith depends from start to finish. (Hebrews 12:1, 2, NEB)

My brothers, what use is it for a man to say he has faith when he does nothing to show it? Can that faith save him? Suppose a brother or a sister is in rags with not enough food for the day, and one of you says, 'Good luck to you, keep yourselves warm, and have plenty to eat,' but does nothing to supply their bodily needs, what is the good of that? So with faith; if it does not lead to action, it is in itself a lifeless thing. (James 2:14-17, NEB)

# 1   *Is Faith Possible Today?*

ON THE NINTH DAY OF APRIL, 1945, DIETRICH Bonhoeffer was hanged in a German prison, for his opposition to Hitler. He was only thirty-nine years old, but already he had made a name for himself both as a committed, fearless Christian and as a theologian. During the two years he spent in prison before his death he thought deeply about the radically new age of history into which, as he saw it, mankind was moving. Always before, society had rested on religious foundations. Throughout the Western world the moral and legal order was based in Christian suppositions. But these could no longer be taken for granted. People, especially religious people, still talked about God, but their actions were based not in religion but in secular motives and judgments. Even the nation's involvement in war had aroused no religious protest. Instead of leaning on religion as a crutch, man was beginning to stand resolutely on his own feet. Mankind was coming of age. How then could one speak meaningfully of God and Christ in a secular age?

No doubt there was much more in Bonhoeffer's mind than he could crowd into the scanty letters and papers he was able to smuggle out of prison to his friends. Perhaps part of what he did write was lost. We have no way of knowing. But what we have is so profound, and at the same time so paradoxical, that it has teased men's minds ever since; especially his references to "religionless Christianity."

. . . The thing that keeps coming back to me is, what *is* Christianity, and indeed what *is* Christ, for us to-day? The time when men could be told everything by means of words, whether theological or simply pious, is over, and so is the time of inwardness and conscience, which is to say the time of religion as such. We are proceeding towards a time of no religion at all: men as they are now simply cannot be religious any more. . . . How can Christ become the Lord even of those with no religion? If religion is no more than the garment of Christianity—and even that garment has had very different aspects at different periods—then what is a religionless Christianity?[1]

These words have been widely misinterpreted. It has been assumed that Bonhoeffer was thinking about a world without *faith*, a world in which personal commitment would be unknown. But he himself was a deeply committed person, and he counted allegiance to God the one indispensable source of strength. In one paper he reviewed the experience of ten years' involvement in the political and moral struggles of his nation, during which almost every support had given way.

Who stands his ground? Only the man whose ultimate criterion is not his reason, his principles, his conscience, his freedom or his virtue, but who is ready to sacrifice all these things when he is called to obedient and responsible action in faith and exclusive allegiance to God. The responsible man seeks to make his whole life a response to the question and call of God.[2]

When Bonhoeffer spoke of *Christ*, or of *Christianity*, he had in mind *commitment to Christ* in this sense of "obedient and responsible action in faith and exclusive allegiance to

[1]Footnotes begin on page 167.

God." When he spoke of *religion* he was thinking of the visible presence of the churches as part of the social fabric and life of the nation—"the garment of Christianity." Religion in this sense includes the organizational structures of the churches, the status and functions of the clergy, liturgical practices, theological formulations, religious art and architecture, rites and observances, and the place all these have in the habits of the people and the life of the nation. And it includes these factors not only as they are today, but as a heritage brought down through history by successive generations of worshipers. It is a cumulative tradition, enshrining the past and building upon it, changing somewhat as each generation emphasizes congenial elements and allows other parts to fall into disuse. This process is visible and describable. It is what we properly mean by "a religion," whether we use the term with reference to Christianity, Buddhism, Islam or any other religious tradition. Bonhoeffer has performed a great service in sharpening the distinction between *religion,* which is visible, and *faith,* the inward disposition of the soul, the basic committed allegiance of the person, which is invisible. We start with this distinction because it is basic to all that follows.

If Bonhoeffer had lived he might have had second thoughts about the term "religionless Christianity." For a living faith can be communicated only through patterns of words and actions that attempt in some way to express worship and commitment. These patterns constitute a religion, whether they are hallowed by generations of use or whether they spring spontaneously from an overwhelming new experience. Faith always clothes itself in a religion, just as life always clothes itself with a body. But there is a valid distinction between the *spiritual energy,* which is faith, and the *visible forms* that make up any of the many religions of mankind.[3] We will make that distinction throughout this book.

Bonhoeffer's viewpoint stemmed from a clear recognition that to vast numbers of people the Christian tradition no longer seemed important or even meaningful. Faith would have to find new garments. It would have to learn to speak in the language of secular thought, the only language modern man is willing to listen to, or is even able to understand. Religious terms—even the word "God"—would have to be restated in the language of relationships that people knew and understood, instead of in the metaphysical terms of traditional theology. He proposed to write a short book to do this. We have the outline, tantalizing in its brevity. The second chapter was to deal with "the real meaning of the Christian faith." It begins:

(a) "Worldliness" and God.

(b) What do we mean by "God"? Not in the first place an abstract belief in his omnipotence, etc. That is not a genuine experience of God, but a partial extension of the world. Encounter with Jesus Christ, implying a complete orientation of human being in the experience of Jesus as one whose only concern is for others. This concern of Jesus for others the experience of transcendence. This freedom from self, maintained to the point of death, the sole ground of his omnipotence, omniscience and ubiquity. Faith is participation in this Being of Jesus (incarnation, cross and resurrection). Our relation to God not a religious relationship to a supreme Being, absolute in power and goodness, which is a spurious conception of transcendence, but a new life for others, through participation in the Being of God. . . . God in human form . . . man existing for others, and hence the Crucified. A life based on the transcendant. . . .[4]

Bonhoeffer was trying in this passage to restate his own faith in terms of this world, the world in which secular man lives and moves, and which he thinks he understands. This is the realm in which science and technology operate, the world over which men have gained spectacular mastery in recent years. That mastery has been gained by hard-headed insistence that facts are facts, and that nothing is to be accepted as known truth until it has been tested. People who think this way are not likely to put much stock in "religious" talk about some other realm that no one has ever seen; they are likely to dismiss it as idle double-talk— "incompetent, immaterial and irrelevant" to the business of living. They want to know whether an affirmation is supported by evidence. Is it tangible? Can it be verified? They ask whether it is significant. Does it help us understand our experience? Does it help us accomplish something? And they ask whether it is true in two respects: Is it consistent with the rest of what we know? And does it work in practice?

It may come to some people as a shock to suggest that questions like these *can* be applied in the field of religion. Following the lead of Bonhoeffer, Christian thinkers and writers of the new generation have been trying to do just that; and they are succeeding. More than that, they find that faith has no need to depend on outworn phrases and habits of thought, any more than the church—God's people in the world—needs to claim special privileges in society. Liberation from either kind of dependence is all to the good.

But the prospect of freedom can be terrifying. In the year 1956 Pastor Marc Boegner, the greatly beloved senior statesman of the French Protestant Church, spoke in Geneva on the occasion of the fiftieth anniversary of the disestablishment of the churches of France. He recalled that in

1906 he was a young minister, newly out of seminary, in his first pastorate. It was with a feeling akin to terror that he faced the prospect of no longer receiving a salary from the government, as all the clergy had done up to that time. Would they all starve? Could they expect their congregations to support them—something French Christians had never been asked to do before? But, he said, in retrospect it was clear that disestablishment had in fact liberated the churches from bondage to the state. In standing on their own feet they had come to maturity and grown in strength. Moreover, being independent of government policies they could speak and act according to the dictates of their consciences with a freedom they had never enjoyed before.

What is happening in this latter half of the twentieth century is a sorting out of identities and relationships that have long been confused. Since we are in the midst of this process it is not easy to think—or to write!—clearly about it. It is a pervasive process, ranging from the individual's fundamental faith allegiance, at one end of the scale, to church-state relations, human rights and the meaning of freedom at the other end. The vast number of subjects dealt with at the Second Vatican Council shows that the process of "updating the church" touches almost every aspect of life and society. And it is a worldwide process, not only because Christians are everywhere but also because social change is reshaping the whole world and cutting away the underlying assumptions of every religion. There is no point in discussing the encounter of the faiths in terms of yesterday. We must try to see the faiths in the flux and tension and radical uncertainty of today and tomorrow.

Furthermore, our concern is practical. We are not interested in knowing how the various religions of mankind measure up to some arbitrary, abstract scale of values. We want to know how far they are able to meet real needs of men and women and of society in the new world taking shape around us. Because religious faith is concerned with the deepest meanings and values of life, it is fair to assume a relation between the religion of a people and the texture and quality of their society. In the chapters that follow we shall look for such relationships. In this chapter we shall examine the relation of faith to personality and society, and in turn relate these two factors to the revolutionary changes of our time.

## THE NATURE OF FAITH

Man has been religious from the time he became man. The earliest evidences of prehistory indicate religious practices, particularly in respect to the burial of the dead. As we approach the beginning of recorded history these evidences multiply. Myth and legend, which precede history, invariably link the living community with divine ancestors or other beings of more than human stature. There was never a time when men and women did not look to the realm of the transcendent—the unexplainable mystery of being, within which the known world of time and space and human existence is set like a small island in a great sea.

This awareness may well have grown out of the wonder with which prehistoric people viewed the world of nature— the star-filled sky, the recurrence of day and night, the cycles of sun and moon, the fruitfulness of the earth and the mystery of human life and death. Anyone who has ever spent a summer night under the stars has certainly shared the feeling of the Hebrew poet who wrote:

> O Lord, our Lord,
>   how majestic is thy name in all
>     the earth! . . .
> When I look at thy heavens, the
>   work of thy fingers,
>   the moon and the stars which
>     thou hast established;
> what is man that thou art mindful
>   of him,
>   and the son of man that thou
>     dost care for him?
>
> (Psalm 8:1, 3-4)

The Apostle Paul regarded both creation itself and the bounty of the earth as evidence of the existence and goodness of God, evidence by which God had declared himself to all mankind. (See Acts 14:17, Romans 1:20.)

The *Rig-Veda,* the oldest religious text of India, contains a reference to the creation, which is, characteristically, in the form of an unanswered question rather than an affirmation:

> The gods are later than this world's creation. Who
>   then knows when it first came to being?
> The source of this creation, and whether one formed
>   it all or did not form it,
> He, who surveys from highest heaven, verily, He knows,
>   Or—perhaps—he does not know.[5]

Faith is the first fruit of man's wonder. It is *recognition* of a reality that man cannot fully grasp because it transcends the reach of his mind and senses. But it includes more than recognition; faith is *commitment.* Religious faith can rise to confident and joyous trust in a God who is love; it can also include courageous acceptance of the doubt and loneliness and even terror with which one accepts the hiddenness of God. It was not lack of faith but a plumbing of the depths of faith that led Job to say, "Though he slay me, yet will I trust in him," or that echoed in Jesus' cry from the cross: "My God, my God, why hast thou forsaken me?"

Faith is a sharing of purpose. "Our wills are ours to make them Thine," wrote Tennyson. The faith reference becomes the basic factor in guiding a person's choices and decisions, and thus in determining what he is, what he does and what he becomes. Thus faith shapes character and personality. Faith itself is invisible. No one else can directly know or see the tie that exists between a man and his God (or his gods, if they are less than God). But the *effects* are visible. We cannot see magnetism, but we can see the compass needle drawn to the north. Nor can we see energy until it reveals itself in its effects on matter in the form of motion, heat, chemical reaction or light. So, too, the basic commitment of a person's life leaves an indelible stamp on his personality.

Faith is much more inclusive than specifically Christian or specifically religious faith. For every person there is at any given moment *one* interest, *one* value that outweighs all others. That to which an individual gives himself most unreservedly is the object of his ultimate concern and commitment. It may be self, or family, or success, or the pursuit of truth and knowledge. It may be God, or the nearest approach to the unknown God that a person is capable of. If the ultimate is *really* ultimate, that is, if it points in the direction of God, faith leads to character and the fulfillment of life's potential. But commitment to a false ultimate can mean that life will became misdirected and futility will set in. Among those who have sensed this most deeply is the late Dag Hammarskjöld, whose diary contained the following entry:

I don't know Who—or what—put the question, I don't know when it was put. I don't even remember answering. But at some moment I did answer *Yes* to Someone—or Something—and from that hour I was certain that existence is meaningful, and that, therefore, my life, in self-surrender, had a goal.

From that moment, I have known what it means "not to look back," and "to take no thought for the morrow."

Led by the Ariadne's thread of my answer through the labyrinth of Life, I came to a time and place where I realized that the Way leads to a triumph which is a catastrophe, and to a catastrophe which is a triumph, that the price for committing one's life would be reproach, and that the only elevation possible to man lies in the depths of humiliation. After that, the word "courage" lost its meaning, since nothing could be taken from me.

As I continued along the Way, I learned, step by step, word by word, that behind every saying in the Gospels stands *one* man and *one* man's experience. Also behind the prayer that the cup might pass from him and his promise to drink it. Also behind each of the words from the Cross.[6]

If faith is the first fruit of man's primeval wonder, the will to understand and to dominate nature is the second. The creation story in Genesis declares that God commanded man to fill the earth, subdue it and have dominion over it. Certainly man has been eager to obey this commandment. But the very possibility of dominating nature depended on the presumption that the universe is orderly. Effects follow causes in a predictable way. Discovery of the laws of nature has been a process of "thinking God's thoughts after him." Making use of them for human purposes is—or should be—an act of stewardship in which man the user cooperates with God the provider. It is here that faith and scientific technology should meet, for both rest on an abiding trust in the orderliness of the universe. If the whole cosmos displays order and harmony—as it does—one creative intelligence, one divine purpose, must be at the heart of it.

But if the universe is one, and its Creator God is one, is there an underlying unity behind the seeming diversity of men's faiths? Certainly God has been conceived in many different ways. Not everything said about him can possibly be true. But that is not the question. Faith in God is not saying something *about* him. Whatever we said would be less than the whole truth. One must trust oneself *to* him. The question we must be ready to face is whether every reference to an ultimate reality, a supreme God, refers to the same God. Because we believe that he is one, the Creator, the Father and Lord of all mankind and of Jesus Christ who gave his life for all mankind, the presumption is that he is the attracting force behind every sincere faith reference. It is understandable that Christians in Europe and America, in their anxiety to safeguard the uniqueness of Jesus Christ, have not always been willing to concede this identity. But Christians of Asia and Africa are bolder, even though they have to meet the fallacious argument that all religions have equal value. The late Toyohiko Kagawa put the matter in a parable based on the old Japanese proverb: "Every way leads to the goal; every religion is good. Do not many paths lead to Mount Fuji?" This proverb refers to the various pilgrim paths to the summit, with their stations along the way, which are climbed annually by thousands of pilgrims. Kagawa said:

Buddhism, Omoto, Tenri, and Islam, all of these religions are good. All contain truth and guidance. But some stop at the sixth resting place on the mountainside, some at the fourth and some become tired and rest even before they have passed the first station. Many rest at the second and some reach only the third. Buddhism may bring us to the ninth resting place, but because it stops there I do not choose Buddhism. I choose Christianity because I want to climb to the top.[7]

## FAITH AND SOCIETY

So much for the purely personal aspect of faith. What is its significance in the shared life of society and nation and world?

First of all, the *group* of people fired by a common purpose because they share the same commitment is immensely important. The band of disciples gathered about a prophetic leader constitutes such a group. "Where two or three of you are gathered together in my name, I am among you," said Jesus. The solidarity of a common commitment is the foundation of effective group action. Every leader knows this and acts on it.

At the level of clan and tribe and nation the sense of a group allegiance has always been particularly strong. Myth, legend, tradition and history are taught and invoked to maintain a sense of shared nationhood. It is, in fact, this feeling of unity that makes a nation. Questions of language, government and political organization are secondary. But religious unity has throughout history, until very recently, been regarded as the principal bulwark of the nation. The myths and traditions have been religious in content, giving the nation the mystical identity of a common supernatural origin. Codes of law and social custom were sanctified as the commandments of the gods. Priests and rulers confirmed each other's authority. Kings ruled by divine right, and the established religion was protected and supported by the state.

The existence of a common tradition, shared by all, gives a nation or people a psychological unity and identity that continues from age to age. The tradition defines its relation to other peoples round about and to past events.

Out of the stream of historical happenings it distills a thread of meaning for the instruction and guidance of succeeding generations, thus shaping the national character and molding value judgments. It underlies the national consensus as to right and wrong, good and evil, loyalty and treason.

This national consensus has a tendency to be a strongly conservative force. It sanctifies the status quo and regards change as destructive. So for the very health of society there must be some counterforce tending toward renewal, change and correction. And because the status quo is ordinarily supported by religion, the counterforce also needs the dynamism of faith to prevail.

Time and again the counterforce that has broken through the rigidity of a static society has been the creative individual, the pioneer, the innovator, the prophet. To break with the established order is not easy. It requires immense courage, the kind that is born of committed faith. The pioneer is often convinced that he is being guided and sustained by a force mightier than himself. He senses that ultimate truth is expressing itself through him, that life itself flows through him. It is not surprising that this sense of power communicates itself to those about him, or that both he and they are convinced that a prophetic word has been given and received.

This phenomenon does not appear only in past history. It happens today. Instances of religious prophetism abound, especially in Africa. But we should realize that the experience is not confined to the realm of religion. It can occur wherever a creative individual, working against opposition, struggles to express the gift that is in him.

To the established order the creative spirit is always troublesome, and innovation is upsetting. The new passes judgment on the old and finds it wanting. Jeremiah, for example, stated his mission in devastating terms:

> Now the word of the Lord came to me saying . . .
> "See, I have set you this day over
>     nations and over kingdoms,
>   to pluck up and to break down,
>   to destroy and to overthrow,
>   to build and to plant."          (Jer. 1:4, 10)

A person who believes he is charged with such a mission will not be a comfortable citizen to have around. He will be a "controversial figure." He will suffer, and so will others. But persons of this stripe are absolutely essential to the health and renewal of society. The tension between what is and what is to be is the force that keeps humanity from stagnation and despair. "Where there is no vision the people perish." It is not to be assumed, however, that the innovator is always right. Even the fact that he gathers a large and loyal following does not mean that his insight is valid. There are doubtless more mistaken prophets than deliberately false and lying prophets; but even one who is mistaken in the substance of what he says may be worthy of honor and respect for his integrity, courage and devotion to the common good.

It is not the task of the prophet or pioneer to provide a road map of the unknown future, but rather a signpost pointing away from the "broad highway that leads to destruction" and toward the narrow footpath of freedom and hope. By themselves, neither the prophet nor the upholders of the status quo can claim a monopoly of truth and wisdom. It is the creative tension between them that engenders constructive change. For faith is not sight but insight. It does not provide the certainty of things seen but the confident hope of that which is still unseen. It is movement toward an uncharted road, a pilgrimage of hope. As Nels Ferré says: "It is an offer to try a kind of life that no one can ever live for anyone else." [8]

From age to age there is need for a succession of innovators and prophets. Society is always in need of judgment, correction and renewal. Furthermore, as Jesus pointed out, the prophet who is stoned in his own generation is often honored subsequently; but honoring the person may take the place of heeding what he said. Unpleasant truth can be nullified by taking it into the liturgy of religion, setting it to music and repeating it over and over until the meaning of the words is forgotten. So new prophets are needed to jar the people awake once more.

I have been trying to describe the tension between the status quo and the prophetic innovator, between forces of stagnation and renewal, in general terms that would apply to almost any society. This pattern is certainly not found only in the Judeo-Christian tradition, or only in the nations of the Western world. Other historic figures, religious and secular, fit the role of prophet. Every society has been threatened repeatedly with stagnation under an entrenched establishment or a static tradition, and every society has been offered new perspectives by unique individuals. Such creative geniuses initially stand within the cultural heritage of their place and time. But they bring into it something fresh and new, something universal, which marks the beginning of a process of change that continues and grows far beyond their own lifetimes. Every great movement of the human spirit, including both the religious faiths of mankind and secular alternatives to religious faith, bears the mark of such originators, though not all are known to us by name.

Among all these pioneers, Jesus Christ is preeminent. To say that he stands at the center of history is not a pious exaggeration; it is the sober judgment of competent historians who see in him not only the culmination of Jewish history but the point of convergence of all the currents of his time. In fact his life first convinced men that the story of man is neither a meaningless jumble of events nor an endless round of recurrent cycles, but a pattern in which order and purpose can be seen.

In *The Meaning of History,* Erich Kahler writes thus of his coming:

> We need no revelation to see in this event a comprehensive result and at the same time a beginning. In it past, present and future are sharply distinguished, and yet vitally connected. The new faith produced a first clear *awareness of the new, of total newness* which is the essence of uniqueness. A nēw world has emerged, not a renewal of the same, as in the recurrent aeons. A "new creature" was proclaimed to have arisen, and the human being appeared changed, and therefore changeable. The church fathers were the first violently to reject the cyclic view.[9]

All the trends that converged in the *time* of Jesus would not have been significant apart from the *fact* of Jesus. It is he who fuses them into wholeness. The coherence of nature testifies to the Creator. The physical world is a cosmos, not a chaos, because he so ordained it. The coherence of history, centering in Jesus Christ, enables us to see a thread of continuity and meaning running through the story of man. We believe that this meaning relates to all mankind in every generation.

In our time as never before, all the separate histories of the nations are fusing into one history. From this time onward the story of mankind will be told as one story. Every people will be able to draw on the heritage of all peoples for anything it chooses to call its own. Jesus Christ thus becomes, at the least, one of the great prophetic figures who will be known and revered by all mankind. How much more than that he will be depends on the degree to which men and women everywhere are moved to commit themselves to him in faith. This commitment rests with him and with them, not with us. But what does rest with us is the obligation to let him be seen and known for himself, and not to insist on our interpretations of him. The Asian or African understanding of Jesus may be quite different from our Western conceptions of him, but no less authentic on that account. As an Indian writer puts it, men will find meaning and hope "in the unexplored regions of our Lord's life and not in the regions already mapped out."[10] In so doing they will confirm once again the experience of every generation of disciples. For Jesus is still out in front, as in that moment so vividly recounted in Mark: "They were on the road, going up to Jerusalem, Jesus leading the way; and the disciples were filled with awe. . . ." (Mark 10:32, New English Bible) No one has overtaken him or fully and completely grasped all that he means to mankind. The Apostle Paul speaks of not having attained but of pressing on to gain "the righteousness which comes from faith in Christ, given by God in response to faith." (Phil. 3:9, NEB) Every man of faith and every church must be continually "pressing on" to grasp more fully and express more truly the present meaning of his life, his words, his trust in the God whom he called Father.

Hence the encounter that concerns us in this book is not an encounter between *religions,* with the Christian churches lined up on one side and the non-Christian traditions of belief and worship on the other. It is the encounter between *faiths,* between obedient commitment to Jesus Christ as Lord, through whom and in whom God makes himself known to men, and all the alternative commitments open to people anywhere. Whether a person or a religious body bears the name Christian or some other name is not the primary question. The real question is to what extent they manifest the mind and spirit of Christ and are open to transformation and renewal by fresh encounter with him.

So also the proper object of mission is not the multiplication throughout the world of churches patterned on those of a particular Christian tradition, be it Protestant, Catholic or Orthodox—a tradition encrusted with history and only partially meaningful today. It is rather the implanting in every place and every culture of "cells of faith and witness," that is, groups of Christian disciples living in creative tension with the society about them, not as foreigners but as full participants in the common life, and yet at the same time as those who live and act under the impulsion of Christ's limitless, outgoing concern for others. Every Christian congregation in the world should be such a cell of faith and witness. Only through such active Christian witnessing presence can a genuine encounter take place.

In the chapters that follow we shall try to comprehend the significance of Christ for the faiths, and the implications thereof for our obedience and our witness as Christians. We face this task in the context of the secular revolution now in full tide.

## FAITH AND THE SECULAR REVOLUTION

The rapid change of our time has been so much written about that no extended discussion is needed. We are living in a revolutionary age, at a significant turning point of human history. Some people find this exhilarating and look forward with hope, while others feel insecure and desperately anxious. To Christians this is a time for confident trust that the tides of history are in God's hands, and for creative response to a new situation. Yet it does raise new and critical questions as to the possibility of faith. The new world culture that is emerging is founded on essentially secular presuppositions. Chapter 4 will deal with the issue of secularization. We turn now to two other aspects of change, communication and technology, which also raise important issues for faith.

## *Communication and Truth*

With the coming of air travel and radio the cultural isolation of former generations has been wiped out, and with it the facile assumption that one's particular way of looking at things is the best way. Values now have to be put to the test of inherent truth or usefulness or attractiveness. The material values and the technical knowledge of the West are finding ready acceptance throughout the world; and a world culture, based on the Western model but enriched by Asian and African arts and skills and cultural values, is emerging.

But what of faith? Is there one "true" faith for mankind? Is there one *most valid* apprehension of God and response to God? Or is each faith so bound up with a particular culture that its "truth" is true only in the context of that culture? In that case what faith, if any, is relevant to the coming world culture? Here the distinction we have made earlier is important. Each *religious tradition* is part and parcel of a particular cultural tradition. None of them is universal. But the *faith insights* that they enshrine *may* reflect one reality. The various quests for ultimate meanings that gave rise to the religions of men may be parts of the same quest. If so, some insights will prove to be more significant than others and will eventually win acceptance by their inherent truth.

What is "truth" in relation to faith? It cannot be mere utility—adequacy for man's needs—for that would reduce ultimate reality to the measure of man, which is absurd. On the other hand "truth" cannot lie far out in the realm of abstract theories, because we have no way to test such theories. They are too ethereal to be helpful. "The Kingdom of God," said Rudolph Bultmann, "cannot be . . . a colorful realm of fancy to which the individual can flee for refreshment and escape from responsibility." [11]

In the simplest possible words, we accept as true whatever enables us to say: "Yes, that is the way things really are." *Truth is a word that matches experience.*

As a result of rapid travel and radio communication, the range of human experience now accessible to us is vastly greater than ever before, and confusing in its richness. We can find many partial insights, many words that match segments of experience; but is there a word that relates the whole human situation to ultimate reality? Can we in fact say: "Yes, this is the way things really are"? Christian faith affirms that such a word has been given to mankind in Jesus Christ, "the Way, the Truth, and the Life."

Truth has a further range of meaning, though, which is suggested by the Greek word for truth, *alethia.* Literally *alethia* means "not forgetful," "not drowsy." Truth is wide-awakeness to the inwardness of things. It is alert responsiveness. It goes on from saying, "Yes, I see that that is the way things really are," to say, "Well then if things are that way, I must think and act accordingly." Truth is more than knowing. It is perceiving *in order to make decisions.* Truth satisfies the mind and challenges the will, and the proper response to it is action.

Truth has still a third dimension: It points the way to further truth. We often find that when we act on the best insights we have, our way becomes more and more clear as we go along. Implications open up. New possibilities beckon that could not be seen or even suspected until the first step was taken. Truth is prophetic, pointing ahead into the unknown. The whole history of science bears out this principle, and it is no less true in the realm of faith. For Christians it has the support of Jesus' assurance that ". . . he who sent me is true, and I declare to the world what I have heard from him. . . . If you continue in my word, you are truly my disciples, and you will know the truth, and the truth will make you free." (John 8:26, 31-32) Thus, in summary we can say that a faith that is true should illuminate experience, elicit active response and point the way ahead.

## Technology and Faith

It is probably no exaggeration to say that more than half of what is now known in the field of science was unknown fifteen years ago. Technologies advance so fast that even specialists in a small field can hardly keep up with new developments. The bewildering prospect of a computerized world frightens us as the thought of witches and demons used to frighten our ancestors. The whole fabric of society seems threatened by new possibilities of psychic control and mass manipulation of people. The balance between human values and technical skills seems to be permanently upset—so runs the dark foreboding of pessimists. Others see in technology a new salvation, the hope of a this-wordly paradise in which man's every material need can be met "from cradle to grave." (But what of death itself? And what of a world crowded to suffocation by an ever-growing population?)

Can transcendent faith survive in such a world? If so, what faith? And what will it offer beyond the satisfactions man is able to achieve for himself? Is religion, for instance, destined to become, even more than it is now, a leisure-time activity—an avocation to fill empty hours, like pitching horseshoes or watching television?

Or will commitment to a transcendent reality enable men and women to realize their true selfhood? Will it suggest goals for the enlarged potential of a technically advanced society? Will it enable men to maintain a perspective of wholeness in which narrow specializations and partial interests are fused meaningfully together? These are long-term issues to which we do not yet know the answers.

The more immediate question is: How is it possible to believe in God in a world dominated by scientific thinking? Isn't God an unnecessary hypothesis? Isn't nature self-contained and governed by its own laws? In other words, doesn't the vastness of the physical universe rule out the possibility of a God who is Creator of the whole cosmos and at the same time concerned about individuals like you and me?

Such a battery of questions deserves far more extended discussion than can be given to it in this book. Positive answers *can* be given. One reassuring fact is that many intelligent people, including many scientists, find that scientific knowledge and faith reinforce each other. The real question is: What *kind* of God must one now believe in? Any little tinkering God who has to be fussily busy keeping the universe running is out; only a "big" God is credible, one who sees it all whole and uses the orderliness of things to give scope for freedom.

When the two teams of astronauts made their first rendezvous in space, some of us found it amazing that the force of gravitation was so utterly dependable that those two vehicles, whirling in space at a speed of thousands of miles an hour, remained precisely in their orbits under the pull of earth and could be maneuvered around each other inch by inch under control of their pilots. It would have upset everything if God had intervened to give them a helpful nudge this way or that. Dependable order is the foundation of freedom to plan, to choose, to act. This is true for man, and presumably for God also.

A mature idea of God is certainly possible for anyone who chooses to "put away childish things." But it demands a willingness to distinguish between matters of primary and secondary importance—for instance, between insights of faith and elements of a religious tradition. One of the most helpful books in reaching a mature view of God is J. B. Phillips' *Your God Is Too Small.* For instance:

. . . If there be a Mind behind the immense complexities of the phenomena that man can observe, then it is that of a Being tremendous in His power and wisdom: it is emphatically not that of a little God. It is perfectly conceivable that such a Being has a moral purpose which is being worked out on the stage of this small planet. It is even possible to believe that such a God deliberately reduced Himself to the stature of humanity in order to visit the earth in Person, as all Christians affirm. But the sort of thing which outrages reason and sets sanity rocking on her seat is to be told that such a God can only operate where there is an unbroken succession of bishops![12]

Or only among the immersed, or the speakers-in-tongues, or the upholders of the Westminster Confession. Or again, only among those who have bathed in the Ganges or gone on pilgrimage to Mecca.

The scale of thinking demanded by "man's coming of age" challenges Christians and men of faith everywhere to grow up. Religious infantilism is a way of escaping reality. It honors neither God nor man.

A mature faith gladly accepts the advances of science and technology as a further step in the dominion of man over the world to which the Creator called him. Every such step enhances the powers in the hands of men, powers that can be used for good or ill. These increasing powers hold the promise of greater freedom and well-being for the whole family of man. But powers used selfishly, without concern for the good of all, cause suffering and bondage instead of freedom. "This is the way things really are." It is the inherent nature of things, the cosmic moral order God has ordained. Human freedom thus carries with it a burden of moral responsibility. Freedom *is* responsibility for the effects of the choices one makes.

We shall see that every great faith has some insight into the cosmic order within which man is placed. There is at least an innate hunger for justice, an instinctive appeal from man to God—or to the gods. But men choose evil rather than good, and so entail the penalties of guilt. Justice demands retribution, and therefore from time immemorial men have stood in fear before their gods. Can the gulf of guilt and fear be bridged? To this supreme question, we believe, Jesus Christ brought the ultimate and final answer. The Christian affirmation is that "God was in Christ reconciling man to himself."

# 2 *Religions of Escape*

AT LEAST TWENTY-FIVE HUNDRED YEARS PASSED between the composition of the following two songs. The first is part of a folk song of pre-Confucian Chinese peasants complaining of harsh tax collectors. The second was sung by Negro slaves in nineteenth century America.

> Big rat, big rat,
> Do not eat my millet!
> Three years have I served you,
> But you will not care for me.
> I am going to leave you
> And go to that happy land;
> Happy land, happy land,
> Where I will find my place.[1]

> Roll, Jordan, roll!
> Roll, Jordan, roll!
> I'm goin' to go to heaven when I die,
> To hear old Jordan roll!

Both songs express the hope and longing of suffering people for deliverance. Such longing has been felt in every age and every land, for when their human situation has offered no ground for hope, men and women have sought " a salvation not made with hands" from some realm beyond earthly existence.

The capacity to hope when humanly speaking there is no hope, and so to keep on living and striving, is one of mankind's most extraordinary characteristics. For many people it is the awakening point of religious awareness, the beginning of faith. It is widespread, if not universal. We find it in Abraham Lincoln, who said, "I have often been driven to my knees by the realization that I had nowhere else to go." We find it in the stress of battle: "There are no atheists in a foxhole." We find it in the spontaneous urgency with which men pray in the presence of catastrophe or extreme anxiety. The hope of salvation, in one form or another, is always a part of religion.

The Book of Jonah makes this point with delightful irony:

. . . there was a mighty tempest in the sea, so that the ship threatened to break up. Then the mariners were afraid, and each cried to his God. . . . But Jonah [who was running away from God] . . . had lain down, and was fast asleep. So the captain came and said to him, "What do you mean, you sleeper? Arise, call upon your god! Perhaps the god will give a thought to us, that we do not perish." . . . (Jonah 1:4-6)

Because Jonah had turned his back on God, he had no one to pray to; so he went to sleep. But doing so made his behavior unnatural in the eyes of all the rest.

It is noteworthy that the term *salvation,* whether used in a religious or a more general sense, always includes the idea of *release* from some threat or danger or burden. It is closely related to the more general term *liberation.* (The English word salvation comes from the Latin *salvus,* meaning safe; liberation comes from the Latin *liber,* free.) From the viewpoint of present-day needs and interests, it is unfortunate that religious concern has centered on "safety" more than on "freedom." In fact this is one of the points at issue between the gospel of Jesus Christ, who died to *set us free,* and the religious preoccupation with making us safe.

While salvation in some form is an interest of all religions, it is more central in some traditions than in others, and the word "salvation" does not always mean the same thing. In this chapter, we shall examine its significance in three great religious traditions in which escape is a primary concern, and in comparable segments of the Christian tradition. The distinguishing mark of this kind of religion is that *it tends to isolate the individual in a world of private concern,* and so is less than constructive in the social order.

## ANIMISM

In our highly literate sophistication, we are likely to identify religion with the possession of sacred books of Scriptures. But men were religious long before they knew how to read and write. Even today, there are many peoples who are only now becoming literate, but there is none whose culture has no religious content. The concepts and modes of worship in which religious feeling is expressed vary enormously from one people to another; yet similar patterns do recur, because mankind is essentially one. There is a unity of nature within the diversity of imaginative response to the unseen.

Hence, it is not totally misleading to use the single word *animism* to embrace the vast domain of preliterate religion, though it is more accurate to speak of the peoples involved as *animists.* Strictly speaking, there are as many different animisms as there are animists—just as there are as many philosophies as there are philosophers—since no two people think and feel exactly alike. Neither religion nor the underlying commitments of faith can be reduced to statistical averages without loss of the highly specific and personal reality we are trying to understand. The danger of turning our attention from people to some abstract "-ism" as if it were a thing in itself will always be with us, but it is more acute in the case of animism because the religiousness of preliterate men and women pervades the whole of their lives.

Animists do not distinguish between "religious" and "secular" aspects of life. Indeed, they do not distinguish between animate and inanimate forces in the world about them. Or, at least, they do not draw the line of distinction where we do. For the animist, life is everywhere. He has no other way of accounting for movement or change or unpredictable occurrences. Knowing that his own actions reflect his will and his intentions, he naturally and logically attributes will and intention to the powers of nature that surround and act upon him. The pattern of his thought and action, his way of explaining the world, rests on the assumption that the forces of nature are living powers.

Explaining the world, however, is not enough. Man by his very nature seeks to dominate the world by understanding it, in order to use its resources for his own ends and control its forces for his own security. Wherever he perceives systematic regularity, as in the alternation of day and night and the recurrence of the seasons, he learns to count on that regularity and make use of it. This realm is the impersonal one of scientific technology; and even preliterate man is often skilled in this domain. But there remains the enormous realm of the unpredictable, peopled, in the animist view, by living powers whose capricious actions can never be relied on. Since they cannot be controlled, the best course is to placate them by sacrifice and carefully performed ceremonial acts. The religious rites of animistic peoples often have this end in view; and as they aim to preserve the well-being of the community in its totality from present danger or threatened evil, the religious and secular aspects are completely interfused and inseparable. To talk about animistic *religion* as if it were a thing in itself is to miss its very nature.

Because the world of the animist is full of dangers, he dare not face it alone. His life is bound up in the common life of family and clan and their extension into tribe or nation. He hardly thinks of himself as an individual; he is primarily a member of the community, which in principle if not always in fact is a kinship group united by descent from a common ancestor. This community is a living fellowship that transcends the life-span of its members. It includes the ancestors, long dead but still venerated, whose help in times of crisis is implored and gratefully acknowledged. It may include yet-unborn generations. Hence those now living regard themselves as trustees of the common heritage of their people, standing under obligation toward those yet to come. This sense of duty toward others, on which the very life of the kinship group is felt to depend, seems to be the source from which flows all the mutuality, all the sense of moral obligation, on which any human society is based.

There are many forces in nature, some helpful to man, others seemingly hostile. These can be regarded in two different ways. Some are personalized as separate spirits or gods. Others are regarded as manifestations of a single energy or soul-force, which might inhere now in one place or object, now in another. This power, called "mana" by the Polynesians, is greatly feared because it can harm or kill. It is also sought as the source of good fortune, success, and authority. The possession of mana "in themselves" accounts for the courage of the warrior and the magical powers of the sorcerer.

The fear of mana gives rise to *taboo,* the necessity of avoiding contact with holy (mana-filled) objects or persons, or of abstaining from certain actions that could release the dreaded power. In many societies, elaborate systems of taboo are used to enforce public order and security. (Is the practice of swearing witnesses on the Bible in our law courts a survival of taboo?)

The effort to escape these forces and turn them to account gives rise to magic, and to specialized practitioners of magic, or *shamans:*

In many primitive societies there are people who are part-time religious specialists, shamans, functioning more or less on their own. Their approach to the spirits is usually quite direct: by hysterical identification, by becoming the voice of the god, or by calling up the spirit of the dead. . . . The shaman believes that he has received his power from a direct encounter with the spirit or god. . . . [He] usually works directly with a single person or a small group on the basis of an agreed fee. . . . He must divine the cause of sickness, prescribe the cure, ward off the attacks of evil spirits, track down witches, counter magic with magic. If he is paid enough by the proper persons, he may himself be induced to play the role of the sorcerer. It is just this double role of the shaman which makes him such a power for good or ill.[2]

In the final analysis, however, the disposition of the spiritual powers cannot be guaranteed—in effect, no one is secure. Thus fear is endemic in animistic society. Faith, in the sense of a trustful relationship to the divine reality, hardly exists because animists are not aware of any *reliable* power at the heart of existence. Animistic cultures that make any reference to an ultimate "high god" almost invariably say: "He is far away, and we know nothing of him." Because the gospel brings assurance of a God who is trustworthy, Christianity readily attracts converts from among animistic peoples.

Every people has to provide for the transmission of its culture from generation to generation. Where writing is unknown, memory is all-important. Priests are carefully trained in the exact performance of ritual; and often the whole community performs dramatic songs and dances together. Narrators and genealogists memorize the annals of the clan or nation. But the chief reliance is on myth. Myth is neither history nor allegory. It is, rather, an expression, in easily remembered narrative and symbolic form, of any group's deepest insights into its own origins and the meaning of its existence. By transposing the story to the remote past, myth gives it the sanctity of immutable truth.

This is at once the strength and the weakness of myth. For to maintain such sanctity, the human order must be unalterably preserved. Any deviation from the demands of the sacred myth would mean the destruction of mythical and religious life. Primitive religion cannot tolerate any freedom of individual thought.

Yet the circumstances of life and the needs of society do in fact change, and sooner or later the fact of change challenges the fixity of social tradition. Ancient myths lose their authority, if not their meaning. Then:

There arises a new dynamic form of religion that opens a fresh perspective of moral and religious life. In such a dynamic religion the individual [innovative] powers have won the pre-ponderance over the mere powers of stabilization. Religious life has reached its maturity and its freedom; it has broken the spell of a rigid traditionalism.[3]

We have deliberately spoken of preliterate religion in the present tense, although in fact the last preliterate cultures are fast losing their coherent identity under the impact of modernization. But animism is not finished. It survives as the deeply embedded substratum of all religion and underlies all cultural developments. Astrology, good luck charms, elaborate funerals, trust in omens, spiritualism and fortune telling are but a few of the present-day descendants of animistic practices. Infinitely more significant are the basic convictions that the world of space and time is not the whole of reality, that life is a unity death cannot destroy, and that man must always seek by all the means at his command to come to terms with the powers of the spiritual realm. Finally, there are the gifts of myth and myth making and the ever-recurring tension between sacred tradition and creative insight. These are the legacies of preliterate man to all the generations that follow. They are the point of beginning for any understanding of the great historic faiths, including Christianity.

## HINDU RELIGION

In the second millennium before Christ, between three and four thousand years ago, the first Hindu sacred texts were recorded and the emergence of the world's oldest major religious tradition began. It seems fairly certain that many of the hymns comprising the *Rig-Veda* had been handed down by oral tradition for centuries before they were put in written form, for they were in such archaic

Sanskrit that later writers had difficulty in understanding them. By 600 B.C. three other *Vedas* had been added, and these four books constitute the basic scriptural authority of Hinduism. They are revered for their form as well as their content, and recitation of chosen verses is regarded as a means of concentrating the mind on the Supreme Being.

In the *Upanishads,* which concluded the Vedic literature, the earlier texts were expanded and expounded, and the impressive structure of Indian religious philosophy began to take form. This was of special interest to the priestly class, the Brahmans, who were also responsible for the correct performance of religious rites on which the maintenance of the whole cosmic order of the universe was believed to depend.

During this period, and indeed throughout Indian history until very recent times, most of the people remained illiterate, and animistic beliefs and practices continued to flourish in a great variety of forms. Thus it came about that there were two distinct levels of Hindu religion, the Brahmanism of the elite and the popular cults of the common people. As time passed these cults were enriched by the developing Brahmanic culture; and in later centuries they were further modified by Muslim, Buddhist, Jainist, Christian and other influences.

Popular Hinduism was given some measure of coherence by the great epic stories of Rama and other heroes, who are regarded in Hindu mythology as *avatara* ("descents") of the god Vishnu. Vishnu preserves the world and sends helpers when evil forces threaten to overwhelm mankind. The *Bhagavad-Gita* (composed about 300 B.C.) is the greatest of these epics and the most important single document of Hinduism.

The common factor that pervades all Hindu culture is its underlying assumptions about the nature and destiny of man. These basic axioms are so deeply held that they are hardly conscious and are regarded as certain beyond any possibility of doubt or question. They center in the twin principle of *dharma* and *karma*.

*Dharma* is the nearest Hindu equivalent to the Western term "religion," but it is much more inclusive. It is duty or righteousness, whether in the legal, moral or religious sense. It is the path a person should follow in accordance with his nature and his station in life, particularly in terms of the privileges and obligations of his caste.

*Karma* is retribution. It is implacable cause and effect applied to the moral realm, the belief that all actions have inescapable moral consequences in this life or a future one. Karma burdens the soul with the effect of past deeds, so that one carries from life to life a stock of merit or demerit which causes unending rebirth.

As implied in this definition, Hindu culture rests on belief in reincarnation. But the ultimate aim and hope is *moksha,* or release into oneness with the ultimate reality, Brahman, conceived as pure Being, Consciousness, and Bliss. As an eminent Hindu scholar, D. S. Sarma, explains, because *moksha* cannot be obtained within the span of a single lifetime, Hinduism provides for a series of lives for each individual, and for the continuity of the self throughout the series. Only so is it possible to imagine justice for those who die without having attained the goal, or for those who by the accident of birth must overcome unfair handicaps.

The doctrine of reincarnation gives a cloak of cosmic morality to the harsh inequities of the caste system. Since no one can remember what he was or did in a previous incarnation, a person has no ground for complaint if suffering or privation is his present lot; and no one need be greatly worried about the poverty or pain endured by others, for it all represents the working out of the inexorable law of retribution. Belief in *karma* and active outgoing social concern are hardly compatible.

Through the doctrines of *dharma* and *karma,* religion has been used to sanctify the world's most rigidly structured society. In Vedic times there were four social classes: priests, warriors, artisans and farmers, and laborers. The latter were the Dravidian inhabitants of India who had been subjugated by the lighter-skinned Aryans. Caste distinctions may have originated in color differences; at least *varna,* which means "color," is used for "caste" in such terms as *varnadharma* (caste law, or social obligation). The four major classes have proliferated into some three thousand caste groups, distinguished by occupation, locality, religious practice or other identifying marks. Each has its place in the social scale with sharply defined rights and duties. In addition there were until recently a great number of outcastes who were excluded from all the privileges of caste and endured a precarious marginal existence on the fringe of society. A person is born into a particular caste and cannot change, though the relative position of the caste group as a whole may advance or decline, a fact that may involve its members in bitter struggle with competing groups.

The great value of the caste system was the stabilization of society in a pattern of complementary duties and responsibilities that made the village a coherent, largely self-sufficient unit. Mr. Sarma evaluates caste in these terms:

. . . during all those centuries when a strong central government was either nonexistent in the country or was frequently changing hands, it was the theocratic ideal of the caste system that saved the Hindu society from disruption. . . .

However, it must be admitted that in the very act of saving Hindu society the system became far too rigid and exclusive and lost all its old elasticity. In the name of the caste system the Hindus have developed too much of class hatred and too little of the spirit of cooperation. The caste system with its rigid walls of separation is bound to pass away, as it has become completely out of place in modern world conditions. But the underlying principle of *varnadharma* [social obligation] is valid for all time, for in the ideal society wealth, numbers, and power should be subordinate to character and culture; cooperation should take the place of competition; and there should be an organic relation between men's aptitudes and their occupations. . . . The most responsible positions should be occupied by the men spiritually most advanced, irrespective of the caste into which they may have been born.[4]

With these aspirations for an ideal society, we can most heartily agree. The question is whether Hindu religious ideas can promote the realization of the hope. Does the Hindu conception of spiritual progression lead to responsible involvement in society? In rare individuals it may do so, but its central thrust is in the opposite direction. It stresses disinvolvement from the world; it is purely individualistic and devoid of social concern. The ultimate aim is escape not only from the bondage of the flesh but also from the limitations of finite being. It includes detachment from the changing world and absorption into the unchanging reality, which endures forever.

Hindu philosophy holds that as far as circumstances permit the life of the individual should embody a spiritual progression, beginning with study and proceeding through active life as a householder and citizen to meditative retirement and finally to complete renunciation of the world as a wandering *sannyasin,* entirely devoted to the service of the Superior Spirit.

Of course only a very few ever carry out these four stages in their entirety, but spiritual progression to some level is within the reach of everyone through discipline *(yoga)* and devotion *(bhakti).* The mystic may be able to apprehend reality as Brahman, the impersonal absolute; and he may see his own existence as an expression of that same absolute. To those for whom such mystic faith is too ethereal, there is offered the other face of Brahman, in which he is "the great Lord of Lords, the great God of Gods, the Master of masters, greater than the great, the adorable Lord of the World." Thus one of the *Upanishads* describes him as "superintending all natural causes, from whom all this rises and to whom it returns." And for those who need a still more approachable deity, there are innumerable gods and goddesses, all of them regarded as manifestations of the One Supreme Being.

In support of this eclectic view, Hindus quote a Vedic text: "Reality is one; sages speak of it in different ways." Historically this tolerance made it possible to absorb all the animistic cults of India into the Hindu fold. (In theory every religion of the world could be brought under the umbrella of Hinduism.) But it also perpetuated belief in the existence of a host of local animistic gods, even among people who also acknowledge one supreme deity. And it precluded any critical appraisal of religious faith and practice, or any consideration of the relevance of religion to life. By discouraging conversion from one religious allegiance to another, even within Hinduism, it tended to bind everyone to the cult into which he was born. Thus it carries the ultimate implication that an individual's religious orientation has no practical significance in the affairs of this world. Worship is reduced to a purely private and individual concern. In conventional Hinduism there is no congregational worship and little sense of fellowship. The Hindu's *puja* (worship sacrifice) is performed alone, in the heart of the temple, where there is a small room without outside light, symbolizing the essentially inner nature of Hindu worship. Indeed, there is room enough at the shrine for only a very few people at any one time.

The Vedic prayers reflect this highly individual concept of worship. For example:

Let the Supreme Being come to me, let the sweetest bliss come to me, may that sweetest bliss, which is the Supreme Being come to me. O Supreme Lord of spiritual knowledge, of your offspring, I am a child dear to you. O you who terminate this nightmare of transmigratory life, stamp out all misery. O Lord of spiritual wisdom, my vital breaths which are thine, I offer as an oblation to you.[5]

In the realm of personal ethics the Hindu Scriptures set a high ideal, with emphasis on such virtues as fearlessness, purity of mind, sacrifice, uprightness, truth, freedom from anger, gentleness, modesty and steadfastness.

If the Hindus have anywhere distinguished themselves it is in their special emphasis on truth, nonviolence, sacrifice and renunciation, which according to them are not merely passive virtues, but represent active social morality. . . .
Nonviolence, ahimsā, is the cosmic outlook of the Hindus which teaches them to respect all life, indeed all god's creation. Closely allied with it is the teaching that man should see with equality everything in the image of one's own self and do good to all creatures. It is indeed well said that the doctrine of ahimsā, with its host of implications, is of far greater importance than the costliest philanthropic institutions.[6]

Unquestionably the principle of nonviolence, especially

as it was developed and applied by Mahatma Gandhi, is a contribution of the greatest importance to mankind. But this and all other ethical insights need to be set in a context of active social concern, which is foreign to traditional Hindu thought. Hindu teaching does not attempt to involve man in the world and its affairs; it aims to detach him from the world. In the *Bhagavad-Gita* it is said: "Therefore, without attachment perform always the work that has to be done, for man attains to the highest by doing work without attachment."[7]

Beginning early in the nineteenth century and continuing to the present time, a succession of pioneering leaders have developed reform movements within Hinduism. In part the purpose has been to absorb into Hinduism the values of Christianity, Western culture and especially British liberal idealism. In part the movements reflect an awakening social consciousness. In part they embody Indian nationalism. Whatever their original aims, the struggle for national independence and a sense of identity as a nation has increased their strength and significance. They tend to exalt Hinduism as the national religion, while at the same time attempting to overcome the mutual antagonism of the many Hindu sects by emphasizing the principle that all religions are fundamentally one. For communalism is the enemy of the united nation-state, just as fatalistic acceptance of *karma* is the enemy of the energetic social action required for nation building. The attempts to revitalize Hinduism are thus motivated at least as much by the need for a bond of national coherence as by any sense of need for a valid religious faith.

Whether such a revitalization is possible, and whether it can come about quickly enough to serve the needs of the people of India at this turning point in their history, who can say? Traditional Hinduism has never come to grips with social issues; it has not been concerned with the actual life of men and women in this world. Its view of reality is not consistent with belief in a Creator God, especially a God who is concerned about the world and who purposefully involves himself in human affairs. It has never conceived of man as capable of creative activity or of cooperating with (or retarding) the fulfillment of God's purpose in creation.

In this crisis there are two alternatives. Either the *faith* of India's people will be shattered because their religion is inadequate, or their faith will reorient itself so as to release a new dynamic into personal and social life and produce a religious renewal. This is the point at which the good news of Jesus Christ bears on India's crisis of faith.

## BUDDHIST RELIGION

In the course of the centuries a number of other religions have arisen as offshoots of Hinduism. The most significant of these is Buddhism. Siddhartha Gautama, the originator of Buddhism, was born in north India about 560 B.C. He belonged to the warrior caste and according to legend was brought up in luxury, shielded from any contact with disease, old age or death. When at the age of twenty-nine he encountered these miseries for the first time he was so shocked that he left parents, wife and child to become a wandering monk. Hinduism was in a stage of active ferment at the time (toward the close of the Vedic period), and Gautama sought help from many teachers. He practiced extreme asceticism in the effort to solve the riddle of birth, life and death, hoping to escape the treadmill of *karma* and transmigration. For six years he found no satisfaction. Then one day in a flash of insight he perceived that salvation lay not in striving but in renouncing existence. From thenceforth he became the Buddha, "the Enlightened One." He set forth his doctrine in simple form, and spent the next forty-five years wandering about India, teaching his way of salvation. Thus Buddhism from the beginning was imbued with a missionary spirit and was popular rather than aristocratic. It was in a sense a layman's revolt against the priestly exclusiveness of the Brahmans.

Gautama accepted *karma* and reincarnation, but he emphatically rejected the Hindu gods. He insisted that the universe operates purely by cause and effect. With no god to appeal to, prayer and sacrifice became meaningless, so he rejected the whole ritual apparatus of the Hindus and referred to the Brahmans as "a string of blind men leading the blind by means of blind tradition."

He asserted that men must work out their own salvation without looking for any help from higher powers. Salvation consists in breaking the chain of causation so as to "blow out the candle of being" and attain *nirvana,* the bliss of nonbeing. The way to achieve this is to overcome desire through knowledge and renunciation.

Basic is the doctrine of the "Four Noble Truths": 1) that all life is inevitably sorrowful; 2) that sorrow is due to craving; 3) that it can only be stopped by the stopping of craving; and 4) that this can only be done by a course of carefully disciplined and moral conduct, culminating in the life of concentration and meditation led by the Buddhist monk.

All things are composite, and . . . all things are transient, for the composition of all aggregates is liable to change with time. . . . Being transient, they have no eternal self or soul, no abiding individuality. And . . . they are inevitably liable to sorrow. This threefold characterization of the world and all that it contains—sorrowful, transient, and soulless—is frequently repeated in

Buddhist literature, and without fully grasping its truth no being has any chance of salvation. For until he thoroughly understands the three characteristics of the world a man will inevitably crave for permanence in some form or other, and as this cannot, by the nature of things, be obtained, he will suffer, and probably make others suffer also.[8]

This is the teaching of a man who faced the harsh realities of existence with unflinching realism and utter commitment to truth. It is amazing that at that point in history he could so clearly grasp the principle of cosmic order in which effect invariably follows cause by the inner nature of things. Nearly two thousand years were to pass before science confirmed that intuition. Furthermore Gautama avoided the trap into which some modern behaviorists have fallen by recognizing that men are never completely bound by predilection and circumstance but always have a margin of choice. Men can always say "no" to desire and thereby change the course of events.

Following the example of certain Hindu sects, Gautama organized his fully committed followers into communities of celibate monks and nuns detached from the world and devoted to meditation. The less committed remained in the world, where they could not lead the perfect life of detachment but could receive instruction and improve their *karma*. Even a devoted layman might enter *nirvana* at death.

Although the Buddha was skeptical about the existence of deity, he himself soon became an object of worship. As the movement spread it developed into many sects within two main groupings. Southern or Hinayana Buddhist sects, which advanced into Ceylon, Burma, Thailand and the whole of Southeast Asia, remained relatively close to the original teaching of Gautama. Mahayana Buddhism originated in northeast India and was more strongly influenced by Brahman thought. It sought the ultimate salvation of all living beings, especially through the self-sacrificing concern of those who have gained *nirvana* but postponed entering the state of blessedness in order to contribute to the salvation of others. These "saints" or *Bodhisattvas* figure prominently in the Buddhism of China, Tibet, Mongolia, Korea and Japan. Some of them appear to have been historical figures, while others are purely legendary. They present a deeply spiritual conception of self-sacrifice, which has given rise to devotional literature of a high order. In northern Buddhism, the Buddha himself is exalted above all gods.

Where Buddhism encountered animistic peoples, as in Japan and Thailand, it usually gained acceptance and became a dominant cultural force. But where it encountered sophisticated, literate peoples with highly developed cultural and religious traditions, Buddhism never became completely dominant. In China it became one of "the three religions" held in common by most Chinese until the present revolutionary era, the others being Confucianism and Taoism. In India, the land of its birth, Buddhism was gradually reabsorbed into Hinduism. Because Gautama's original insights are congenial to certain schools of "scientific" agnosticism, Buddhism has recently aroused interest in the Western world.

Buddhism today forms the substratum of East and Southeast Asian culture, much as Christianity forms the substratum of Western culture. It has endowed its adherents with a sweetness of disposition, a resilience and gentle firmness of character, a tranquil gaiety, which are striking to the foreign observer. Thus John V. Taylor, visiting the Garden of Emptiness near Kyoto early one morning, watched Japanese students and young people come to meditate and asked himself:

Is it only the superb artistry of the old Zen designers who laid out the garden 500 years ago that draws aside so many of Japan's youth from the throb of her teeming industrial cities? Or do they come out of their agnosticism and meaninglessness to try to learn from these silent rocks how to welcome the ultimate annihilation with peace of mind?[9]

Japanese culture is basically Buddhist, but it has been reinforced by Confucian ethics with a strong emphasis on social obligation and by the religious nationalism of Shinto. Under the shock of military defeat and disillusionment after World War II there have emerged several "new religions" based in Buddhism and Shinto, which together claim several million members. These zealously promulgated cults promise health, security from disaster (such as earthquakes), peace in the home and the solution of social problems. Thus they are this-worldly variants of the age-old Buddhist concern for salvation.

In the less-industrialized countries of Southeast Asia traditional monastic Buddhism is dominant. The monks are often the most highly respected men in the community. Their brotherhood is one of the few coherent, organized social groupings—sometimes the only one. Therefore, by necessity they have assumed leadership in movements of national liberation and become active in politics—roles entirely foreign to traditional Buddhism. Vietnam provides the most obvious instance, but the whole region faces the same need for leadership in this time of change.

Thus the peoples of Buddhist tradition, like all men everywhere, find themselves drawn inevitably into a new world situation, a new culture, for which the past offers little precedent or guidance. Simply to renounce the world is not enough; for mankind has a claim on the gifts and capacities of its members. The infinite compassion of Buddhism has meaning for today, but it must be a compassion that results in positive, constructive action. There is no spark to kindle the flame of action in the view that the world is sorrowful, transient and soulless, as Buddhism affirms. Jesus Christ affirms the opposite: that this is God's world, that he loves mankind, that his purpose is eternal, and that he is able to turn sorrow into joy. Will Christ provide the spark to kindle the latent flame of Buddhist compassion?

## INTROVERTED CHRISTIANITY

Escapist salvation-seeking is found among Christians, too, and has all too often vitiated the life and witness of the church. In the early centuries some ardent Christians felt impelled to go out alone into the desert to wrestle with their sins, instead of bearing their part in society and in the corporate fellowship of the church. Through the centuries Christians have tried to assure their own salvation by rigorous moralism, by ascetic practices, even by the pursuit of martyrdom. Neither the practices themselves nor the idea of gaining salvation thereby find any warrant in the New Testament, but anxiety to escape the imagined terrors of hell and gain the felicity of heaven has often been the dominant motive of Christian preaching. To cleric and layman alike, this was what the gospel was about. Little else mattered.

Actually there was always more: the outpouring of charitable concern for those in need, the relief of suffering, attempts to assure justice for the oppressed and to curb the oppressor—such expressions of the social dimension of the gospel have recurred throughout Christian history. In the dark centuries when European civilization was at a low ebb, the monastic communities provided centers of ordered life, of learning and teaching, of healing and relief and social reconstruction, without which society would have reverted completely to barbarism. But all this was a by-product rather than a conscious aim of the monastic movement.

With the rise of highly individualistic modern culture during the past two hundred years, concern for private salvation has been marked—especially in North America, where emotionally charged revivalism matched the mood of frontiersmen, pioneers and empire builders. As the nineteenth century progressed, the idea that the church should confine itself to saving souls and keep out of such practical affairs as business and politics became increasingly popular.

We thank God that this attitude is now decisively rejected by the leaders of the churches and by a major proportion of the members as well. The emasculated "Sunday go to meeting, weekday go the way of the world" version of church membership was too hypocritical, too patently fraudulent to command the allegiance of serious people much longer. In becoming involved once more with people in all their struggles and suffering, the churches are again finding their own souls—they are rediscovering their calling as servants of Jesus Christ. This is meaning. This is mission.

Yet such involvement, carried to excess, may also degenerate into a religion of escape. Busyness may become a facade hiding emptiness of soul. We may work feverishly to escape the necessity of thinking, of facing reality, of listening to the inner voice which is the Spirit of God. Supporting good causes may be a way of compensating for a sense of unreality in worship and a loss of conviction about the hidden mysteries of God. Doing for others may be a substitute for the word of assurance we can no longer speak with sincerity.

But escape into activity is not by itself the answer to doubt. Doubt is part of faith, because faith involves reaching out beyond the tangible, the known—even the knowable—to that reality which mortal mind and spirit can never fully grasp. "Faith gives substance to our hopes, and makes us certain of realities we cannot see." (Hebrews 11:1, NEB) Work and contemplation are both part of the Christian way. Study and discussion, meditation and prayer, corporate worship and the sharing of experience go hand in hand with active involvement in society and witness through work well done. Either aspect by itself reduces Christianity to a religion of escape; both kept in balance give it wholeness and healing power.

## SOCIAL IMPLICATIONS OF FAITH

A time-worn definition asserts that "religion is what a person does with his solitariness." This statement is largely true of religious traditions that conceive salvation in terms of escape, whether it be escape from malignant spiritual forces, from retribution and reincarnation or from the torment of a guilty conscience. To the extent that religion sets an individual apart from others in a private world of his own, in search of a purely private, individual salvation, it misses the way. For in fact, "no man is an island." The individual achieves wholesome personhood only through growth in mutuality, in sharing and serving and living in fellowship with other people. A religious system that neglects this dimension of life has little to offer, especially today when the whole world is growing together into a single, complex, deeply interrelated family of man. Authentic Christianity is uniquely significant at this point, because it sets the person in the context of the universal human family, and it proclaims a God who chooses to be addressed as "Our Father."

A true faith commitment, as over against a merely formal religious affirmation, draws the faith-led person into a new obedience that tends to make him increasingly like the object of his faith. The response of a faith-filled person is not abstract but concrete. It relates to the particular circumstances of time and place in which he finds himself, the persons around him, the social order of which he is a part, and the choices open to him as an individual and as a participant in family, community and nation.

For those who have been touched by the spirit of Christ, whether or not they are formally identified with the church, one of the most transforming aspects of this faith response today is the steadily expanding awareness of the social dimension of the gospel. According to Jesus the first and greatest commandment is this: "The Lord your God is the only Lord; love the Lord your God with all your heart, with all your soul, with all your mind, and with all your strength." (Mark 12:29-30, NEB) But to this description of the absolute commitment of obedient faith, Jesus added: "The second is this: 'Love your neighbor as yourself.'" (Mark 12:31, NEB) In our day the instruction, "Love your neighbor" is being recovered from neglect and from sentimentality. It is being seen as a strong, masculine, all-encompassing directive that leads to our involvement as

God's servants in every human struggle for liberation from evil or crippling limitation, with whatever suffering may be entailed. Step by step and year by year the variety and extent of involvement grows. Churches and their members are engaged today on frontiers of social struggle that were not even imagined a generation ago. And as experience grows, so does competence. No thinking person would pretend to have all the answers to the ills and dangers of present-day society; but those who serve under the impulsion of love for others, and who offer all their gifts of heart and soul and mind and strength, are the most likely to gain mature judgment and lay sure foundations.

## CONVERSION AND PERMEATION

In every part of the world today, including Europe and America, committed Christians are a minority in a largely pagan society. In each of these societies Christ presents himself as a living challenge to the status quo. Where there are no deeply entrenched religious establishments, for example, among animistic tribes, many people find in him the Light and Truth they have not known how to discover for themselves. As one African woman said on hearing the gospel story: "I always knew there had to be a God like that!" As a result the church often grows rapidly among such peoples, and its members contribute much to the restructuring of society and to cultural adjustment during the period of change from preliterate tribalism to modern nationhood. This has been particularly true in many parts of Africa.

In the ancient nations of Asia the impact of Christianity has been less dramatic. Relatively few Hindus or Buddhists formally embrace Christianity and become members of the churches. The churches are present in Asia in considerable strength, but their membership is drawn largely from the humble, depressed segments of the population. Because this *is* true it tends to *remain* true; persons of wealth or social distinction are not attracted to a body which has no prestige and which seems alien to the national culture. Sometimes the church members fall into the "ghetto mentality" of a despised minority and withdraw into a shell of separateness. In caste-conscious India, for example, it is hard to avoid such self-isolation.

Yet permeation is taking place. The New Testament is widely read. Eminent Asian leaders acknowledge their indebtedness to Christ even while they remain steadfast in their own religious heritage. Thereby they help open that tradition to change from within. Two Westerners recently visited every Buddhist agency of social welfare in a great city of Southeast Asia. In every instance they found that some Christian influence had prompted or stimulated the undertaking.

One overhears an Indian saying: "Jesus is the only divinity to whom I pray." Christians may shrink from the thought of Jesus becoming just another member of the Indian pantheon—but will it come to that? How can Hindus generally come to know him other than by starting from the religious conceptions they now have? Paul did not hesitate to identify the God whom he proclaimed with the unknown God whose altar he noticed in Athens. It is quite possible that a man who feels drawn to pray to Jesus will soon perceive that he speaks a word and offers a hope that none of man's traditional gods can provide.

For, in the last analysis, Jesus Christ challenges the ancient religions of Asia not so much at the level of conscious beliefs and practices as at the far deeper level of underlying presuppositions. They rest on the principle of *karma*—retributive justice that works itself out inscrutably through many cycles of reincarnation. Jesus Christ reveals a God of mercy who cancels retribution by his own forgiving love, who takes upon himself the burden of man's sin and offers in its place the yoke and burden of responsible freedom. Asians of many faiths have at times glimpsed this ultimate liberation; but their religious traditions have had no place for it. So the differences are real and must be faced. The late Paul Devanandan, who was Director of the Christian Institute for the Study of Religion and Society at Bangalore, India, defined the task of Christian communication in these terms:

The Christian apologetic for our times in India is best set forth not so much in defence of the Christian position as in explanation of the difference between the Christian and the Hindu understanding of religious fundamentals. What has been done in this regard has become out of date, and does not adequately meet the demands of the present situation. Three things call for attention in this matter of Christian apologetics. One is that it should take account of the varieties of Hinduism and deal with them separately. The second is that we need to clarify the religious terms used interchangeably by the Christian and the Hindu in philosophic, popular and village religious categories. This in itself is the best explanation that we can give of corresponding Christian concepts, to indicate just why and where we claim to differ from our Hindu friends. The third would be the more daring task of discovering in the process the place and possibility of an Indian Christian expression of the faith committed to our fathers. . . .

. . . New India in the making is in desperate need of a unifying principle that will provide a living bond of national coherence. . . . Our national leaders are contending that this unifying culture would and could emerge from a synthesis of what can be retained from the traditional past and what can be absorbed from the revolutionary present. This cultural ferment presents us with both an opportunity and a challenge.

What is called for is a sense of profound humility. . . . Pretensions to scholarship and research can be self-defeating unless there is consuming devotion to Christian commitment. It is not the vain desire to justify ourselves as Christians before our Hindu kinsmen, but the eager anxiety to explain the inadequacy of our Christian witness which has perplexed and confused them, that should set us to this study of contemporary Hindu religious beliefs and practices. For we believe, "Not that we are sufficient of ourselves to think anything of ourselves; but our sufficiency is of God; who also hath made us able ministers of the new testament; not of the letter, but of the spirit: for the letter killeth, but the spirit giveth life" (II Cor. 3:5-6).[10]

# 3 Religions of National Identity

WHEN THE PATRIARCH ABRAHAM LEFT UR OF the Chaldees he became the spiritual ancestor not only of the Jews but of the Christians and Muslims as well. His pilgrimage of faith "looking forward to the city with firm foundations, whose architect and builder is God" (Hebrews 11:10, NEB) was the watershed between the individualistic polytheisms of Asia and the covenant monotheism of the peoples of God which was to take form in Palestine, Arabia and the Western world. In Hinduism and its offshoots, each man stands alone under his burden of *karma*. Alone he aspires to salvation and seeks release from the chain of being. In the Judeo-Christian-Islamic tradition, the person finds meaning and dignity in being a member of a people or nation which, corporately, stands in a covenant relation with God because God has taken the initiative and opened the way.

Of course many nations besides these have used religious terms to confirm their sense of national identity. One of the political parties of India defines a Hindu as "one who recognizes India as his motherland and his holy land." The ancestor cults of many peoples exalt the earliest ancestors to the status of the gods and thus unite the nation by mythical ties of divine descent. Japanese Shinto has this character. It asserts that the ancestral gods created the Japanese people separately and endowed them with unique, superior qualities. The greatest of those gods created the islands of Japan in all their beauty; afterward the rest of the world was made from mud and foam. Hence, according to Shinto belief, every Japanese is in spontaneous possession of the way of the God. This kind of belief makes a nation regard itself as set apart from other peoples. Their link with divinity, instead of binding them to other men in a common humanity, isolates them.

The Hebrew prophets had a wider vision. They asserted that the whole world was made by one Creator, and that he is actively concerned for all its peoples. This belief transcends nationalism:

. . . The God who created and guides the people we know is the same God who created and guides the people we don't know. "Did I not bring up Israel from the land of Egypt, and the Philistines from Caphtor and the Syrians from Kir?" says the Lord. (Amos 9:7) It is not that the Chinese are the children of one god and the Americans the children of another. Any such faith as that would cut us off completely from the Chinese, for we would be part of one creation and they would be part of another. Since, however, they are the creatures of the same God who made us, it becomes clear that we cannot be related to *God* without also being related to *them*.[1]

That this universalism stems directly from a faith commitment to God, the Creator of the universe, cannot be denied. It is a principle of vast importance, especially today as barriers fall and peoples are brought into ever-closer contact. But over against it stands the conviction that he chose one particular people as his own. This conviction is the very life blood of Judaism and is hardly less significant to Christians and to Muslims. The conflict of these two opposing principles, universalism and particularism, is the recurrent motif of the whole history of Jews, Christians and Muslims, both in their self-understanding as separate peoples and in the relations between them. Only today are there signs that the age-old conflict may soon be resolved under the combined effects of the secularization of society everywhere, the emergence of a single world culture and a deeper reading of the action of God in history.

We have generally thought of the stories of Judaism, Christianity and Islam as three separate but interlocking histories. In reality they are one history. Perhaps we shall understand them better if we look at them that way, even though there is room in this chapter to sketch only a few highlights.

## HEBREW ORIGINS: THE COVENANT PEOPLE

Now the Lord said to Abram, "Go from your country and your kindred and your father's house to the land that I will show you. And I will make of you a great nation, and I will bless you, and make your name great, so that you will be a blessing. I will bless those who bless you, and him who curses you I will curse; and by you all the families of the earth will bless themselves." (Gen. 12:1-3)

Thus the historians of Israel recounted Abraham's call in words that embrace both the particular and the universal: "I will make of you a great nation . . . and by you all the families of the earth will bless themselves." In their eyes God's promise to Abraham was confirmed by the deliverance of the Hebrews out of Egypt under Moses and their establishment in Palestine as a nation. For centuries their allegiance wavered between the fertility gods of the land and the high God of Abraham and Moses, whose worship centered in the Temple at Jerusalem. It was as the deliverer from bondage that priests and prophets and psalmists

alike proclaimed God. It was in terms of a reciprocal covenant obligating Israel to worship God in return for the
liberty and security of the nation that the idea of mutual
responsibility between God and man took root.

But Israel's national security did not long endure. As
its political fortunes darkened, the vision of the great
prophets grew bolder. If the Israelites, God's covenant
people, were called to suffer, it was not by chance, nor
was it merely in expiation of their failure as a nation to
remain faithful to God. There was a deeper meaning. In
the suffering lay the reason for their calling as a nation.
The "suffering servant" disclosed the nature of God's compassion for mankind, the sign by which all the families of
the earth should bless themselves in Abraham. Erich Kahler
writes:

They suffered one subjugation after the other, and were immediately involved in the rises and falls of the great powers of
antiquity, the Assyrian, the neo-Babylonian, the Persian, the
Hellenistic of Alexander and the Seleucids, and the Roman.
They survived them all by outlasting their physical, political
establishment and evolving into a spiritually global community,
accompanying or sharing the destinies of the peoples of the
world in all their ages until this very day. They survived partly
through the transference of their own particular experience of
suffering onto that of historical humanity: they did not suffer
alone; they were compelled to witness and participate in the
suffering of others. . . . This has remained their form of life
through the millennia—wandering, emigration and immigration,
exile and diaspora, perpetually aimed at an ultimate Land of
Promise. . . .

The projection and complement of this kind of existence was
their concept of the divine: a God, unbegotten, without mythical
genealogy and kinship, without a home place, but omnipresent,
without perceptible shape or name, but with a strongly apprehended impulse and will; indeed pure impulse and will, moving
freely like the wind. He is *one* God, supreme, leaving no room

for others, having no truck with others: . . . a dynamic God, goading and guiding the people, and thereby creating it—hence in retroprojection, a creator of all things.[2]

It was in the writings of the great prophet of the Exile (Isaiah 40-55) that Israel's mission to the nations was most poignantly expressed. Yet a generation later, it was in Jerusalem, where a handful of exiles returned from Babylon struggled to reestablish the nation, that the separateness of "the chosen people" was most bitterly affirmed and enforced. Under Ezra and Nehemiah mixed marriages were dissolved, foreign customs were rooted out, and an attempt was made to build a theocratic state in which only Jews would have a place. The civil law was based on the religious tradition as recorded in the sacred books and interpreted by the religious authorities. However imperfectly it was realized in practice, this theocratic ideal persisted in principle until the destruction of Jerusalem in A.D. 70.

Yet sometime during the post-exilic period the universal mission of Israel was strongly reaffirmed in the book of Jonah. In this biting parable God sends Jonah to warn the wicked city of Nineveh of wrath to come. Jonah does not want Nineveh to be saved. He tries to run away, but God brings him back and reluctantly he goes to Nineveh and preaches. To his own amazement the whole city is converted. All the people—even the animals—repent in sackcloth and ashes. Jonah is angry; he hoped the wicked city would be destroyed. So God asks him: "Do you do well to be angry?" Jonah finds a shady place and sits waiting to see what will happen to the city. But the plant over his head withers, and the sun beats down, and again he is angry. And the Lord said: "You pity the plant, for which you did not labor, nor did you make it grow, which came into being in a night, and perished in a night. And should not I pity Nineveh, that great city . . .?" (Jonah 4:10-11)

Thus, even when Jewish nationalism was in the ascendant, God's concern for the whole family of man was not entirely forgotten. Both conceptions were part of the Jewish heritage, which formed the matrix of Christianity.

## CHRISTIAN ORIGINS: JESUS AND THE CHURCH

Many threads of history and human aspiration drew together at the point where Jesus appeared. One of these was the messianic hope of the Jews. Many Eastern peoples dreamed of a great future king who would restore order and prosperity. Among the Jews it was hoped that a messiah (literally "anointed one") would miraculously free the chosen people from subjection to foreign rule and establish God's everlasting kingdom on earth. Under the harsh Roman rule bands of activists fanned revolutionary enthusiasm while monastic communities like that of Qumran undergirded the popular hope with prayer and study and ascetic discipline. The immediate followers of Jesus seem to have included both types. His teaching, his life and his death must be viewed against this intense popular expectation. Another thread of history was the mingling of peoples that had scattered colonies of Jews across the world from Babylon to Rome and at the same time had made the Greek language and the stoic philosophy accessible everywhere. These were the means by which the good news of Jesus Christ would be able to break out from the shell of Judaism as a new and liberating word from God. A third element was the *pax Romana,* the wide-flung Roman Empire which provided order, stability and open communications. Roman rule provided an enormous area without internal frontiers and so enabled Christians to spread their message rapidly and widely.

Yet behind all these immediate factors lay a deeper one, the age-long God-centered faith of the Jewish people. This must never be forgotten. It was the decisive factor in the Christ event.

There is no measuring the depth of Christian indebtedness to Jews. The transforming truth that God is one; that he is just, that his love outruns his wrath—these are Hebraic insights upon which the positive values of modern civilization rest. From the Jews we inherit the Covenant we share. . . . To them we owe the human matrix in which our Saviour lived. To them we owe the writing of our Scriptures.

To Jews we owe our debt for the human participation in the first establishment of the church. It was Jews who first became Christians. It was Jews who determined to go beyond the Jewish community and carry the Gospel to us Gentiles. It was Jews who determined it was not necessary for a Gentile to become Jewish in order to become a Christian. When as a result, Christianity passed over into the Greek world, it was the Hebraic elements in the Gospel that prevented our faith, humanly speaking, from disintegrating into yet another Graeco-Roman form of religiosity.[3]

It is surely unnecessary to retell the story of Jesus and the founding of the church. Let everyone reread it for himself in its authentic, New Testament form. Yet the very familiarity of the story may weaken its impact on our imaginations. Let us therefore quote Dag Hammarskjöld's arresting portrait:

A young man, adamant in his committed life. The one who was nearest to him relates how, on the last evening, he arose from supper, laid aside his garments, and washed the feet of his friends and disciples—an adamant young man, alone as he confronted his final destiny.

He had observed their mean little play for his—his!—friendship. He knew that not one of them had the slightest conception why he had to act in the way that he must. He knew how frightened and shaken they would all be. And one of them had informed on him, and would probably soon give a signal to the police.

He had assented to a possibility in his being, of which he had had his first inkling when he returned from the desert. If God required anything of him, he would not fail. Only recently, he thought, had he begun to see more clearly, and to realize that the road of possibility might lead to the Cross. He knew, though, that he had to follow it, still uncertain as to whether he was indeed "the one who shall bring it to pass," but certain that the answer could only be learned by following the road to the end. The end *might* be a death without significance—as well as being the end of the road of possibility.

Well, then, the last evening. An adamant young man: "Know ye what I have done to you? . . . And now I have told you before it came to pass . . . One of you shall betray me. . . . Whither I go, ye cannot come. . . . Will'st thou lay down thy life for my sake? Verily I say unto thee: the cock shall not crow. . . . My peace I give unto you. . . . That the world may know that I love the Father, and as the Father gave me commandment, even so I do. . . . Arise, let us go hence."

Is the hero of this immortal, brutally simple drama in truth "the Lamb of God that taketh away the sins of the world"? Absolutely faithful to a divined possibility—in that sense the Son of God, in that sense the sacrificial Lamb, in that sense the Redeemer. A young man, adamant in his commitment, who walks the road of possibility to the end without self-pity or demand for sympathy, fulfilling the destiny he has chosen— even sacrificing affection and fellowship when the others are unready to follow him—into a new fellowship.[4]

By Jesus' acceptance of death on the cross, the new fellowship did come into being. Its strength lay in the conviction of its members that God had raised up Jesus from the dead, and "made him both Lord and Christ" (Acts 2:36), and that the radiance and power which suddenly filled their lives was actually his spirit within them.

Among the many metaphors in which the Apostle Paul tried to express this conviction, two are particularly meaningful. The first compares the church to the human body which "though composed of many members is yet one body," each member serving the whole body in its particular function under the authority of "the head of the body which is Christ." In Paul's imagery the church is the new body of Christ, which had replaced the physical body of Jesus, so that through the obedient response of its members to his directing spirit, Christ continues to live and work among men. Thus the Christians carried forward the mission of the suffering servant "always being given up to death for Jesus' sake, so that the life of Jesus may be manifested in our mortal flesh . . . so that as grace extends to more and more people it may increase thanksgiving, to the glory of God." (2 Cor. 4:11, 15)

The second simile used by Paul relates to "adoption," the "grafting" of the new Israel into the old. Throughout most of his ministry Paul was involved in controversy with those who insisted that Christians must observe the Jewish ceremonial law. Paul insisted that faith in Christ superseded the law, so that Christians came by faith into the same covenant relation with God to which Jews had access by the law. They were the new Israel grafted into the old, children of Abraham by adoption instead of by birth.

At this point the universal implications of the Jews' faith came into direct conflict with their self-awareness as the chosen people. The rift between the two communities widened. Only those Jews who conceived their chosenness in terms of sacrificial suffering, as Paul did and as Jesus had done, could reach across it. For those who thought of chosenness in terms of privilege or divine favor or even national identity, it was impossible to include the Gentile Christians within a new and larger Israel.

Before the question of relationship had worked itself out, catastrophe overtook the Jewish nation. A rebellion against Rome broke out, the Jews were crushed and Jerusalem was destroyed. For more than 1800 years, the Jews were to be a wandering people dispersed among the nations without a homeland of their own. It is only by faith that they have continued to exist—faith that as God's chosen people they still have a special mission to fulfill. Sustained by this strong sense of destiny, they have survived homelessness, enmity and persecution. Driven from city to city and country to country, with no lasting security, often in danger of extermination, especially at the hands of Christians inflamed with anti-Semitic hysteria, they have survived. More than that, they have made creative contributions to the life and culture of all the nations among whom they have lived. No other people has such a record.

Meanwhile the Christians grew from a persecuted minority into a mighty host. With explosive missionary zeal they carried the gospel into every part of the then-known world. As congregations multiplied, church administration developed to keep pace. In competition with all the religions of the ancient world Christians out-lived, out-thought and out-died all the rest. Christianity became the dominant faith of the Roman Empire. But establishment brought peril, for in the fifth century barbarians overran Rome and the Roman Empire lay in ruins. Out of the shattered debris of human hopes and expectations, Augustine, Bishop of Hippo, forged a new interpretation of history as a cosmic conflict between good and evil. His classic *City of God* became the charter of Christian thought and action for more than a thousand years.

When the civil structures of Roman rule went into

eclipse, those of the church remained largely intact. Bishops, especially the Bishop of Rome, thus became involved in affairs of state and even in civil administration. Society in Western Europe became partly theocratic, as it had been in the Jewish state after the Babylonian captivity. "Christendom" came to have a geographical meaning—it included those countries in which Christianity was the religion established by law and custom. But imposition of a religion by law carries a dangerous implication: heresy becomes a crime, dissent is disloyalty. The Christian church in Western Europe forgot its origins as a voluntary fellowship of members drawn together by personal commitment to the same Lord. It became the religious counterpart of the state, compelling the allegiance of all the people. In country after country, time after time, its wrath was turned upon the Jews, to whom disavowal of Christian dogma was an obligation deeper than life itself. Out of those centuries of suffering came the Jewish affirmation of the right of dissent, which in our own day has placed the Jewish people in the forefront among the defenders of human freedom.

The churches of Western Christendom were weak in another way. Being identified with the surrounding culture they tended to lose the critical power of a body with its own separate identity. Since people were born into the church, membership required no act of the will, no personal decision, no commitment of faith. Conformity tended to take the place of conviction. Where church membership is universal it tends to be nominal. The same situation prevails today wherever the church is so identified with "the establishment" that membership is a matter of cultural conformity rather than personal conviction and commitment.

In the East history took a different course. While Rome

declined, Constantinople prospered. As the capital of what remained of the Roman Empire, it was the seat of the Ecumenical Patriarch, the "first among equals" of the heads of the ancient churches in the countries of the Eastern Mediterranean, Asia Minor and the Near East. Substantial Christian communities existed even in Persia and India. Deeply divided by doctrinal cleavages as well as by cultural isolation, the Eastern churches had little cohesion; and like those of the West, they were too much identified with the surrounding culture to exert much force for renewal. The creative energy of primitive Christianity was spent. Into this static situation came Islam, with the shattering force of a new revelation.

## MUSLIM ORIGINS: MUHAMMAD AND ISLAM

The main facts of the life of Muhammad are well known. Born about A.D. 570 in Mecca, he was orphaned in childhood and brought up by relatives. At the age of twelve he began to fend for himself. He seems to have visited Syria with a trading caravan and learned something of both Jewish and Christian beliefs and traditions. He entered the service of a wealthy widow named Khadija, and at the age of twenty-five he married her. Having freedom for thought and contemplation he became deeply meditative. He found a secret retreat in the desert and spent much time there, seeking a clue to the ultimate meaning of life. He saw with increasing clarity that the spirits and djinns whose clamorous worship filled the streets and shrines of Mecca were of no real account. Behind and beyond everything there must stand One alone, Creator, Ruler and Judge of the whole world, who had revealed his will to a succession of prophets from Abraham to Christ. The conviction grew in him that salvation from the futility and confusion of life could come in one way only, through submission to the will of God. So Islam (submission) became the key word of Muhammad's life and teaching.

Submitting himself to the will of Allah (the name is related to the Hebrew *Elohim,* "the Lord") it was borne in upon Muhammad that he himself was called to be the prophet of Allah. The conviction slowly gathered in years of meditation suddenly burst into his consciousness with the force of a revelation. First his wife Khadija, then a few close friends and later a widening circle of intimates heard and believed his story. Finally the word became public. Mecca was in an uproar, for the new movement appeared to threaten the cult of the Kaaba, the great black stone that had been an object of pilgrimage from time immemorial. Muhammad and his little band of supporters were persecuted. Some fled to Ethiopia. In 622 Muhammad and his followers moved to Medina. This emigration or *hijra* (Hegira) marks the year one of the Muslim era.

Already at Mecca the revelations that came to him were being recorded. They became chapters, or *suras,* of the *Qur'an.* This continued at Medina, but the later suras reflect the changing character of the movement, as Muhammad became the spiritual head of a new faith and also a legislator and a military leader.

It is clear that Muhammad regarded himself as standing in the succession of the Hebrew prophets. He expected the Jewish community at Medina to acknowledge him and was bitterly disappointed when they did not. Up to that point the Muslims had faced toward Jerusalem for prayer; thereafter Muhammad bade them face toward Mecca, and he set about making Mecca the capital of Islam.

In the year 624 his followers began to raid caravans of pilgrims en route to Mecca. A series of battles followed, and in the end the Muslims won. The animistic shrines at Mecca were destroyed, but the Kaaba was preserved and became the objective of Muslim pilgrimage, as it is to this day.

This resorting to force brought into the movement a new element—the *jihad,* or holy war of conquest—which continued long after Muhammad's death in 632. An extraordinary combination of military prowess, religious fervor and political skill made Islam both attractive and irresistible to one people after another for more than a century. Who shall say that under the circumstances of that place and time the choice between persuasion and conquest should have been other than it was? Certainly Muhammad himself was changed by it. The man of prophetic vision and insight became a military leader; the preacher of submission to God became a ruler of men.

To later generations the choice seems unfortunate; and at the ultimate level of obligation to the absolutes of every age the contrast between Muhammad and Jesus is inescapable. As Kenneth Cragg has said:

Opposition there was, in Mecca; vested interest, bigotry, sin, and evil. Bearing the brunt of that opposition in single-minded devotion, Muhammad the preacher is a person whose nobility still reaches us through the intervening years. Is the returning conqueror a greater figure?

. . . the Prophet's biography is finally the story of a crucial choice, no less crucial than that implicit in the contrasted Gospel saying: "The cup that my Father hath given me shall I not drink it?" It is the decision arising from the question: "How should Prophethood succeed?" What is the final relation of the messenger of God to the people to whom he is sent when they forebear to hear? The Muhammadan decision here is formative of all else in Islam. It was a decision for community, for resistance, for external victory, for pacification and rule. The decision for the Cross—no less conscious, no less formative, no less inclusive—was the contrary decision.[5]

Thus Muhammad laid the foundations of a great theocratic empire that was eventually to stretch from Indonesia to Spain and from the Balkans to the Sudan. The supreme political power was vested in the caliphate, which continued in unbroken succession until 1924. In the eighth and ninth centuries the caliph's court at Baghdad was one of the great cultural centers of the world. Islam not only preserved the heritage of antiquity during the centuries when European civilization was in eclipse, but it also achieved fresh advances in art, science, philosophy and literature. The Crusades (approximately 1096-1300) were militarily a costly failure and a source of lasting enmity between Muslims and Christians, but they brought Western Europe back into the stream of cultural advance and so prepared the way for the Renaissance.

Religiously, the focus of Islam is the *Qur'an*. In Muslim eyes Muhammad was not the author but merely the transmitter of the *Qur'an*, which already existed in the heavens and was revealed to him, sura by sura, in a state of mystical ecstasy. Therefore the language is sacred as well as the contents. A vast body of commentary has grown up around the *Qur'an*, but only in recent years have Muslim scholars begun to ask themselves what human influences may have gone into its composition. To the non-Muslim the *Qur'an* shows a clear development of style from the early poetic suras to prosaic legal language in the later ones, and a similar evolution of content from prophetic denunciation of idolatry, through exhortation and preaching, to legislation.

Taken as a whole, the *Qur'an* affirms the theocratic principle—the unity of the political state and worshiping community as one and the same. In practice it was always
necessary to make room for non-Muslim religious groups
like the Jews of Medina. To this end Muhammad accepted
the *political* submission of Jews and Christians ("the peoples of the Book," he called them) and allowed them to
maintain their own religious rites and separate civil status
on payment of special taxes. This is the "millet" system,
which still prevails in Muslim lands. It classifies the population into separate religious communities—millets—Muslims
in one, Jews in another, the various Christian groups and
other minorities in still others. Since the Muslim community
is governed by the sacred legal code of Islam, the *Sharia,*
each of the other millets is assumed to have an equally
binding legal and social code, by which its members are
required to live and conduct their affairs. Thus a Muslim
state does not consist of one body of citizens but of several
distinct peoples, each with its own identity, with extremely
high barriers between them. It is always possible to defect
from a minority millet and become a Muslim, but conversion
in the opposite direction is not recognized under Islamic
law, and thus is extremely difficult. And a person who is
not an accepted member of any millet is a social outcast
with no rights and no place in society.

As the giver of the *Qur'an,* Muhammad himself is "the
Seal of the Prophets." In Muslim eyes he is the latest and
greatest of the long succession of those through whom the
One Almighty God has made known to mankind his law
and his will—but not himself.

The *Qur'an* does not use the term "Father" of God nor "son"
of the believer. It allows only *Rabb* [Lord] and *'abd'* [servant

or slave] . . . the substance of what God reveals is His will rather than His nature . . . the end of revelation is obedience rather than perfect knowledge . . . God himself is withdrawn in . . . transcendence . . . [Yet] in its finest form . . . this relation of the '*abd*' to his Lord means a constant quality of consciousness and will unique to Islam. It produces a sense of totality in religion evident in the familiar refusal of the classical Muslim mind to differentiate between sacred and secular . . . God himself is inescapable. Therefore relationship to Him in everything is likewise inescapable.[6]

This transcendent presence is borne in upon the Muslim by the echoing call of the muezzin, "There is no God except God, and Muhammad is the Apostle of God"; the obligation to prostrate himself in prayer five times daily; and the duties of almsgiving, fasting in the month of Ramadan, and pilgrimage to Mecca for those who are able to undertake it. These are the Muslim's tangible responses to the invisible sovereignty of God, which pervades the whole of life. The strength and binding power of Islam is evident in the fact that it numbers some three hundred million adherents today, more than fourteen hundred years after the death of Muhammad.

## BARRIERS TO UNDERSTANDING

The history of mankind for the past 1400 years has thus been marked by the simultaneous existence of three great religions all resting on faith in the same supreme God. That Jews and Christians worship the same God has never been in doubt. There should be no more doubt in the case of Islam. The three faiths differ widely in what they say *about* God. They differ even more widely in religious tradition and practice. (Such differences exist also between branches of the same faith.) But their ultimate faith reference is necessarily one.

Since both Christian and Muslim faiths believe in One supreme sovereign Creator-God, they are obviously referring when they speak of Him, under whatever terms, to the same Being. To suppose otherwise would be confusing. It is important to keep in mind that though the apprehensions differ, their theme is the same. The differences, which undoubtedly exist, between the Muslim and the Christian understanding of God are far-reaching and must be patiently studied. But it would be fatal to all our mutual tasks to doubt that One and the same God over all was the reality in both. Those who say that *Allah* is not "the God and Father of our Lord Jesus Christ" are right if they mean that he is not so described by Muslims. They are wrong if they mean that He is other than the One Christians so understand. . . . predicates about God may differ widely but God as the subject of differing predicates is the same subject.[7]

Yet during many centuries these differing predicates about God have kept men and nations divided into conflicting groups. On all three sides there have been deep sincerity and often sacrificial self-commitment. Men and women suffered for their faith. They felt themselves blessed and uplifted in serving God. Unhappily both Christians and Muslims often believed that service to God involved fighting each other, and Christians through the centuries have shamefully persecuted Jews in the name of the God they both adored.

For on all sides the commitment of loyal faith was equated with dogmatic rigidity of belief and interpretation. If one was right the others were necessarily wrong. To some extent the theology of each of these religions was developed in conscious opposition to the others, and was intentionally defensive and exclusive. They built barriers that were higher than necessary. Thus the *Qur'an* describes the annunciation to Mary in words of reverence and beauty:

Then we sent unto her Our Spirit and it assumed for her the likeness of a perfect man. . . . He said: I am only a messenger of thy Lord, that I may bestow on thee a faultless son . . . that we may make of him a revelation for mankind and a mercy from us. . . .

But then the *Qur'an* adds a limiting postscript:

It befitteth not the majesty of Allah that He should take unto Himself a son. Glory be to Him! When He decrieth a thing, He saith unto it only Be! and it is.[8]

To a larger extent the barriers to understanding derive from the fact that the interpreters of each faith worked in isolation from the others. Each tradition thought of itself as whole and complete; it interpreted its faith without any of the insights and qualifications that dialogue with the others might have provided.

Among the many reasons why such dialogue did not take place, the most important is that the rival faiths were the pillars sustaining rival political structures. For a time Islam and Christendom were opposing empires, and they re-mained the focuses of opposing mass loyalties long after the empires had disintegrated into nation-states. Until very recently it has been assumed that every nation should be sustained by a national religious tradition. The theocratic principle—union of church and state—dominated the worlds of Islam and Christianity. In a negative sense it dominated the world of Judaism also, for the uniqueness of the Jews lay in the fact that they were a nation without a homeland of their own. They alone, of all peoples, had no place in which they could create a state in conformity with their religious tradition.

Even the Protestant Reformation did not immediately bring the theocratic principle into disrepute, though the rise of dissident sects claiming the right of religious freedom began to undermine it even before Luther and Calvin and

Henry VIII broke with Rome. The Reformation leaders claimed the right of religious self-determination on the national scale, but they were not tolerant of dissidents within the nation. The Peace of Augsburg (1555) established the principle: *"Cuius regio, eius religio*—the religion of the ruler is the religion of the state," which was reaffirmed nearly a century later in the Peace of Westphalia (1648). Not until the eighteenth century did the right of private judgment in matters of faith and conscience begin to be conceded in Western Europe and North America. Only in recent decades has religious freedom won recognition as a basic human right. We still have not reached the point where this right is freely conceded in all countries. The old idea that loyalty to one's nation entails an obligation to accept the national religion still prevails over large parts of the world, not least in certain Muslim nations.

Meanwhile Christian missionary efforts among Muslims and Jews were beset by special difficulty, because the missionary and his hearers had extremely different cultural values. As a rule the missionary thought in highly personal terms, and he spoke out of the radical individualism of Western culture. He sought the conversion of individuals, which necessitated a transfer of membership from the very strongly knit Muslim or Jewish community into a church fellowship with totally different traditions, observances and values. Only a very profound faith commitment to God as "the God and Father of the Lord Jesus Christ" could engender this severing of ties and change of allegiance. Relatively few have made the change, and fewer still have withstood the pressures urging them to return. Nor has there been any considerable number of converts to Islam or Judaism from either of the other faiths. Almost complete stalemate has prevailed. Jews, Christians and Muslims worship one God, but they have worshiped from within the cultural contexts of their different historical communities. The common source of their faith has not given rise to a common witness to mankind, but rather to competing and conflicting testimonies. All humanity has been impoverished by this irreconcilable conflict.

Do we now stand on the threshold of a new day in which old rigidities will be broken down and a new consensus of faith may emerge? Strong indications point that way.

## TOWARD CONSENSUS?

We are witnessing today for the first time in history the emergence of a truly pluralistic society, one that does not merely tolerate but actively welcomes diversity in religious faith and practice. In the United States especially, religious pluralism is increasingly recognized as both necessary and desirable. In part, this fact is the result of our national history, which has brought together many migrant peoples with different cultural backgrounds and traditions. We have had to learn to live together, and we have discovered that diversity enriches all of us. A few generations ago the prevailing national philosophy was "the melting pot," and we assumed that immigrant peoples would shed their differences and be assimilated into a uniform American amalgam. This has not happened, and the nation is the richer for it. Within one nation we have many subcultures— groups united within themselves by a bond of a common national origin, a common outlook and often a common religious heritage. We have found that loyalty to the nation and loyalty to the group seldom conflict; they move at different levels.

The First Amendment to the Constitution of the United States established in law the principle of religious pluralism for the first time in history. The Universal Declaration of Human Rights sponsored by the United Nations has extended the principle to the field of international law. The Vatican Council has put the weight of the Roman Catholic Church behind the principle that every man should be free to follow the dictates of his conscience, and that there should be no coercion by civil authorities in matters of faith and religious observance. These three enactments, taken together, mark a turning point in human history from the theocratic principle to the principle of religious freedom in a world community of secular states. We have seen that in many parts of the world these principles are not yet fully understood or accepted. There will doubtless be decades of resistance and many efforts to avoid the challenge they pose to established religion everywhere; but history is clearly moving in this direction. The mobility of peoples and mingling of cultures make religious pluralism a fact even where it is not accepted in principle. Governments are increasingly involved in education, health, social welfare and national development—interests affecting the whole population regardless of religious orientation. Freedom of action in these spheres is incompatible with submission to the dictates of one particular religious community, especially one that looks to the distant past for its style of life.

The whole Middle East—the heartland of Islam and the land of promise of Judaism—is being shaken by the processes of development and modernization in ways much too complex to be described here. Even the conflict between the state of Israel and its neighbors must be passed over without discussion. But the establishment of Israel as a

Jewish state and the simultaneous withdrawal of Pakistan from India as a Muslim state pose the issue of theocracy versus the pluralistic secular state in the sharpest terms. Both are anachronisms, and neither is able to carry out the conception of a religiously oriented nation-state which led to its founding. And both pose serious problems for their co-religionists in other lands.

The separation of Pakistan from India was justified on the ground that only in an Islamic state could Muslims truly be themselves. It was the result of exaggerated communalism. Jinnah, the leading founder of Pakistan, was not personally very religious. He used the idea of an Islamic state as a political device to rally support, but managed to avoid defining what an Islamic state would be in this modern world. Thus he exploited religious zeal for secular ends, using Islam to screen operations that were really motivated by nationalism.

One of the mistaken assumptions had to do with the possibility of achieving a solidly Muslim population. As it worked out, even after the tragic mass migration of Hindus to India and Muslims to Pakistan, 40 percent of the population of Pakistan is non-Muslim, and 40 million Muslims remain in India. Pakistan has not been able to demonstrate an Islamic way of life that vindicates the need for separate existence as a nation. Partition has only bred a lasting and futile bitterness toward India and multiplied the practical problems of modernization and use of resources. Political activism has pushed aside the basic issue of the relevance of Islam, as a religion, to the life and needs of twentieth century men and women. Religious renewal, which had made hopeful beginnings before partition, is no longer in active ferment.

For the forty million Muslims in India, however, the existence of Pakistan poses a dilemma. As loyal citizens of India, they are forced to disavow the principle of the theocratic state, which has always been central to the Islamic tradition. Thus on balance the establishment of Pakistan has tended to undermine rather than confirm the ideal of the Muslim nation-state. Similar trends are evident elsewhere in the Muslim world. Islam as a unifying political force is losing ground before the separate nationalisms of the Muslim states, while the social and political rights of non-Muslims are increasingly recognized.

The state of Israel has had to face the same basic issue of religious establishment in a modern state. Zionist nationalism is considered by some to be little more than a modern political transformation of a traditional religious concept. The motives and expectations of the returning Jewish migrants have varied widely. Some are religious Zionists, to whom the restoration of Zion was the fulfillment of prophecy and the vindication of their ancestral faith. For others Israel signifies a refuge from social discrimination and persecution—a solution of "the Jewish problem" in terms of political emancipation. While the latter group constitutes a clear majority in present-day Israel, their freedom to develop the country as a secular modern state is limited by the insistence of the Orthodox minority that religious observances be imposed by law. The National Religious party plays an important role in politics. Its activity is countered by such movements as the "League for the Abolition of Religious Coercion," and many progressive, forward-looking citizens resent it.

With large-scale help and support from abroad Israel is succeeding as a nation, but as a vindication of the idea of the theocratic state it has not succeeded, and it cannot. The best hope for the future lies in the transformation of Israel into a nonsectarian, open society that can take a constructive and cooperative place in the Semitic Middle East. The desire for just such a transformation is growing among Israeli Jews themselves.

The religiously neutral state and the open pluralistic society thus appear to be emerging as the prevailing pattern for the future. This new situation provides a setting for dialogue between men of differing religious traditions at a level rarely possible hitherto—dialogue with the aim of reconciliation. In a pluralistic society every religious group is free to worship as it pleases (within the limits of public order and decency), to teach and to proclaim its beliefs. Every sincere group is held in respect; none is subjected to coercion or social pressure. All citizens are equal before the law, whatever their religious affiliations. But these principles imply corollaries that are not always spelled out. If every group is to be respected, its members must hold others in equal respect. If each is to teach and proclaim, it must also be willing to listen and to ponder. It must be open, not defensively closed in on itself. Integrity in maintaining truth requires willingness to explore differences together and to accept new truth—even unwelcome truth which corrects or goes beyond what a person has known before. This principle of integrity has been the foundation of man's liberation from ignorance and superstition in every domain. Religion cannot be abstracted from its demands. All the religious traditions thus come together not as antagonists but as searchers and suppliants for the reconciling truth, which God alone can give.

It is too early to predict the outcome of the quest, but a

few points are already clear. One is that allegiance to the truth is not *necessarily* a matter of "either-or"; it may sometimes be "both-and." The first disciples of Jesus did not cease to be Jews in order to become Christians. They were both. Should it not be so today?

> . . . Paul insisted that a Gentile did not have to become a Jew in order to become a Christian. Today we force a Jew to become a Gentile if he is to become a Christian. A Jew ready to re-think the question of Christ is presented today with the socially abhorrent and theologically gratuitous necessity of deserting his own community and joining a Gentile community if he should come to a confession of Christ's messiahship. Is it impossible to think of a fellowship of Christians, both Jew and Gentile, united in faith and mission? Is it impossible to think of an appeal to Jews within their own community that might mean not just the conversion of individuals, but the infusion of the Jewish community—already so rich in fellowship and achievement—with the riches of Christ? Is it impossible to think that thus God might heal the first great schism within the people of his covenant?
>
> As Christians, we dare not hope for less. Individual discoveries of the grace of God in Jesus Christ are always reasons for gratitude. However, Israel has a destiny as a people. It is unthinkable that Israel should be absorbed into our divided churches by the multiplication of individual conversions, and lose the historic identity maintained for three millennia. Our aim should be nothing less than [that] we should be used of God for re-uniting the two separated halves of the people of God.[9]

The same hope may be expressed with equal fervor and conviction in respect to Islam. Of course serious reconsideration of many points of disagreement will be needed. But this no longer looks as formidable as it once did. To cite a single issue: Christians assert the finality of Jesus Christ, while Muslims hold that Muhammad is the Seal of the Prophets. Both terms, it has been assumed, mean "the last in time"; but chronologically only one can be last. Daud

Rahbar, who is deeply versed both in Islamic and in Christian thought, points the way to a reconciliation. The finality of Christ may properly be taken to mean that he alone is ultimately significant and that his significance continues to unfold down the ages.

> The truth is that instead of ceasing, the revelation of God has been established as a continued and eternal and more abundant process after the earthly life of Christ. In all champions of charity, peace, healing and gracious justice, humble or renowned, regardless of creed and race, we must recognize the working of the holy contagion of Christ that has, by the will of the Father of all men, infected countless numbers of the human family. And the observable working of that holy contagion is the continued revelation of Christ. . . . The champions of charity . . . are recipients of the gift of his [Christ's] holy contagion.[10]

As for the Qur'anic phrase "the Seal of the Prophets," one sect, the Ahmadiya, holds that Muhammad not only confirms the message of the former prophets (including Jesus Christ) but is the seal also of the prophets emerging after him. To orthodox Muslims today this is heresy, but there is hope that it may come to be accepted as men become more objective. Meanwhile, argument is less important than the way we live our Christian faith.

> Actually the Church should be dedicated to witnessing to the sovereign Godhead of Christ and the ultimacy of his categorical forgiveness and love as a guarantee of human freedom from fear and hatred of fellow-beings, and fear of earthly calamities and imagined tortures of the next world.[11]

It will not be easy to reach a relationship of open, noncoercive fellowship in which such witnessing and searching together can take place. But faithfulness to our Lord demands nothing less of us. Eugene Smith has well stated the terms of this engagement:

Throughout all this encounter, let there be no religious imperialism. It is never we who open men's hearts to Christ, but the Holy Spirit. It is never we who show the glory of our Christ, but the living Christ himself. He is not an idea which we present: he is a living Presence who continually seeks out every person for whom he died and rose again from the dead. He is a Seeking Saviour who stands at the door and knocks. If we truly seek his guidance in this encounter he will give it. It may well be that he will prompt us for a long time, primarily to listen and to learn; the ill effects of twenty centuries of arrogance are not wiped out quickly. In relations with Jews especially [and, we may add, with Muslims], effective witness to Jesus Christ requires self-emptying and the servant status (Phil. 2:7). We do not dare try to manipulate dialogue with devout Jews [and Muslims]. We can only enter upon it, and together offer it freely into the hands of the covenant-making God whom we [all] worship.[12]

# 4 *Secularism*

FOR A VAST AND GROWING NUMBER OF PEOPLE secularism has taken the place of religion. They do not necessarily oppose religion; they simply ignore it. Their interests lie elsewhere, and religious faith and practice seem irrelevant. Their lives are lived within the tangible world of the here and now. Any other world is, at best, shadowy and unreal. The present world of space and time operates on its own dependable principles of physical causation. It is self-contained, without visible dependence on anything beyond itself.

To be sure, this point of view leaves many questions unanswered. It gives no clue to any meaning or purpose in existence. It points to no ultimate and offers little ground for deciding what is "good" or what is "bad" beyond the immediate interests of the moment. It affords no real basis for a system of values. But the secularist holds that these questions, however troublesome, are vague and imprecise. They cannot be answered with the clear finality of the laws of physics. Perhaps, says the secularist, there are no final answers. But in any case, man must find the answers for himself. They are not given by revealed oracle or divine decree, as something to be "taken on faith" without rational examination and critical inquiry.

This attitude includes an element of true emancipation. The secularist is free from the irrational fears of the supernatural which have often enabled religious cultists to hold sway over the credulous. That realm of darkness is cleared away. Men have succeeded in mastering the physical world by learning to distinguish between real natural forces and the fictitious powers ascribed to gods and demons and magical incantations. By extension of secularist principles into the social realm, men and women of this generation hope that a "great society" responding fully to all human needs can be achieved. This hope is worthy, and the healthy-minded skepticism to which it gives rise is basically sound. Its value is demonstrated by the fantastic achievements of science and technology in our own day. If man can explore the moon and outer space, can he not create a world society immeasurably better than anything we now have?

As a matter of fact, space science and social advance are related. The immense concentration of physical research and creative effort which has made space exploration possible has spilled over into other fields. Mental effort is being applied to every human problem with a new intensity and persistence. In fact *applied intellectual power* is the hallmark of our time. It has become almost axiomatic that whatever man wants to do he can learn to do; and learning how to do things, through research and technological advance, has become a major human activity. In the most advanced countries it commands stupendous resources of knowledge, skill, time and money. Indeed, the more developed a nation is, the greater its potential for further advance; and this growing imbalance constitutes a basic human problem of our time. Technology seems able to provide for every human physical need; it should be able to meet every biological need, including control of the world's population. In the field of human relations and social organization the issues are far more difficult and our technical competence to deal with them far less assured.

Recent studies of bees suggest that the whole hive must be regarded as a single living organism. Individual bees serve one or another of the vital functions, and if one function fails the whole hive dies. If this is true also of human societies, as it seems to be, the task of learning to understand society in order to keep it healthy will be incredibly complex. Yet, the effort is being made and will continue.

The enormous expansion of intellectual power bolsters man's confidence in himself and still further reduces his sense of dependence on God as a power or reality beyond himself. But the process of secularization, of which this is the latest expression, has been going on for a long time and has already resulted in profound changes in society. Politically it shows itself in the emergence of the secular state. In the economic and social realm it burst forth in the Industrial Revolution with its resultant social upheaval, leading to socialism, communism and the continuing social revolution of our time. These are the context of Christian witness today, and are thus all relevant to our theme. But the earliest instance of a humanistic state, consciously organized on rational principles, is found not in the West but in China.

## THE CONFUCIAN STATE

Confucius must be numbered among the great originators of history. Although he lived in an age when primitive superstitions and cultic sacrifices were almost within memory, he sought for understanding through rational inquiry and thus laid the foundation of the scholarly tradition which for many centuries provided China with an elite corps of public servants.

Confucius regarded all creation as a natural order, essentially moral in character. "Heaven," the ultimate power sustaining and governing the world of nature, was also the providence whose will controlled the destiny of mankind. The moral, upright man who fulfilled his obligations toward others would surely enjoy the favor of heaven. The "mandate of heaven" sustained rulers and governors as long as they were wise, just and benevolent; but if they became foolish or corrupt they lost the mandate of heaven and with it the moral authority to rule. (The concept of the mandate of heaven is still current in present-day China.) Confucius believed that the collective experience of mankind would bear out man's spontaneous sense of what is right. Hence the best way to comprehend the will of heaven was to study history and learn from the experience of former generations.

Hence, though Confucius was personally reverent and pious, he rarely invoked divine sanction for his views, but sought rather to base human relations and political organization on rational principles. His writings were little noticed in his own time, but in succeeding centuries they became the basis of a philosophy of government that made the Emperor a cosmic figure, the son of heaven, responsible for the political administration of a huge empire and for the fulfillment of man's being and the harmonious functioning of the laws of nature as well.

There was a period of more than seven centuries (approximately A.D. 220-960) during which the religious conceptions of Buddhism and Taoism were in the ascendant, though the Confucian classics remained the basis of the civil service examination system, which was already firmly established. Chinese Buddhists developed a number of philosophical systems, and more importantly they introduced contemplative and devotional practices, emphasizing faith and discipline, which mitigated to some extent the humanistic cast of Chinese life and thought. But world-renouncing Buddhism gave no guidance in statecraft. An administrative reform in the tenth century gave a new impetus to Confucian studies, and once again social analysis and political philosophy became dominant in Chinese culture. Among educated people, religion and worship receded to a peripheral status and remained there.

Is a similar change of balance taking place in the world today? If so does it embrace the peoples of the Christian tradition equally with Buddhists, Hindus and Muslims? The shape of human civilization for generations to come might be determined by the answer.

Though the Emperor was the all-powerful son of heaven, he was also a man, who might be weak or strong, wise or foolish, feeble of will or despotic. It was therefore necessary to surround the throne with an elaborate system of administrative controls to keep the machinery of government running and prevent abuse of power. Chinese political treatises discuss many problems that reappear whenever large-scale social planning is attempted. It was hard to steer a course between overcentralization of power and excessive diffusion of authority and to maintain a balance between legalism and laxity. It was hard to control corruption. Most of all it was hard to inculcate a sense of responsibility toward the public in local officials who knew they were more likely to be censured for stepping out of line than to be held in high regard for independent judgment and initiative. One report described them as "concerned only in moving with the utmost caution so as to stay out of trouble until they have the good fortune to be relieved of their posts, and . . . quite unwilling to undertake anything of profit to the people."[1]

Yet the extraordinary thing is not that failures and abuses occurred, but that a country as large, populous and diverse as China was able to remain politically united, surviving wars and calamities, for so many centuries. The secret of its coherence seems to have been the institution of the civil service, which steadily drew into the service of the nation an elite class of scholars versed in the Confucian tradition and imbued during the impressionable years of youth with a high ideal of commitment to the public good. Most deeply of all, it lay in the tradition itself, with its faith in a natural order that is also a moral order, in obedience to which man finds his own fulfillment. Time after time, in periods of decline and decadence, scholar-sages found in the classics the incentive and the clue to reform. They were not always able to bring about the renewal they sought. Banishment, imprisonment, torture, even death were sometimes the lot of men who censured corruption in high places. But the tradition of service and faith in the cosmic order lived on. A deposed seventeenth century minister of state named Huang Tsung-Hsi put it clearly:

The reason for ministership lies in the fact that the world is too big for one man to govern and that it is necessary to share the work with others. Therefore, when I come forth to serve, it is for the whole world and not for the prince; it is for all men and not for one family. . . .

The terms "prince" and "minister" derive their significance from service to mankind. If I have no sense of duty to mankind I am an alien to the prince. If I come to serve him without any consideration for the welfare of mankind, then I am merely the prince's menial servant. If, on the other hand, I have the people's interest at heart, then I am the prince's mentor and colleague. Only then may I really be called a minister.[2]

The weakness of the whole system lay in the lack of a unifying sense of nationhood pervading all levels of society. Confucianism was a code for gentlemen, a code based on the principle of *noblesse oblige*. It had little to say to the common people, but left them to find solace in the world-renouncing doctrines of Buddhism or the magical practices of Taoism. Strict Confucianists derided Buddhism as selfish, because it emphasized escape from the burden of existence, and they scorned Taoism as mere superstition. Hence the unity of the Chinese nation was a political unity centering in the imperial structure and administration. It was not undergirded by a deeply felt sense of national identity embracing the whole population, which might have consciously united the people of China into a nation. In the words of Sun Yat-sen, "the people of China are like a sheet of sand." In the end the central authority was unable to adjust itself to the new situation resulting from the penetration of Western cultural influences and commercial interests. Entrenched bureaucracy stifled initiative. National unity and concerted action could not be achieved, and the Empire disintegrated. The nationalist revolution of 1911-1912 overthrew the Manchu dynasty; but before the new leaders were able to achieve national reconstruction China was engulfed in the Communist revolution.

It was during the nineteenth and early twentieth centuries, a time of disintegration, national humiliation and confusion, that Christianity reentered China through the activity of missions. Coming just then it appeared to be merely the religious aspect of Western cultural penetration. And missions were, in fact, one of the great mediating agencies that made the values of Western culture accessible to the Chinese people, both formally through schools and universities and hospitals and the organized life of the churches, and informally through intimate contacts between missionaries and their Chinese associates. Missions thus represented a foundation-laying process of immense importance for the future. The Communist revolution released a violent reaction against Western domination, in which Chinese Christians have suffered greatly. Perhaps only by such a process could the true significance of the gospel for China be disentangled from the Western dress in which it came. It is still too soon to foresee the outcome with any degree of clarity.

## SECULAR NATIONALISM IN THE WEST

We have seen that a common faith has often been the cement that united people into one nation. This has been true particularly in the case of Jews, Muslims and, in times past, of Christians. By contrast the new nationalism of modern times is secular rather than religious in character. It does not depend on a mystique of common descent from a mythical ancestor, or on the religious uniformity of the population, or on the official observance of religious rites. Laws are enacted by a legislative body and not imposed by divine decree. Modern nationalism has been secularized. More exactly, it has been *desacralized,* that is, purged of the imputation of supernatural authority or divine sanction. The state today is regarded as a purely political creation, not as a politico-religious entity.

While this is true in principle, however, it is still not altogether true in practice. Archbishops still preside at the coronation of kings and queens, American coins bear the motto "In God We Trust," oaths are taken on the Bible. Established churches still exist in many countries—Catholic, Orthodox, Coptic, Lutheran, Anglican, Presbyterian—though whether establishment is a boon to either church or state can be questioned. But in any case these elements are recognized as a carry-over from the past and are more likely to decline than to grow in importance. The question is, what will replace them?

Around what secular force can a sense of nationhood cohere? No convincing answer to this question has yet been given. The nineteenth century, especially in Europe, was a period of vibrant nationalism; but it was a nationalism based on fervid mass emotion rather than on rational precepts. Where there was no historic national tradition that could be idealized as a focus for patriotism, the people itself, the *Volk*, was cloaked with a mystical aura of the sublime. Patriotism became the supreme virtue, especially in times of war; and the separate nationalisms were divisive and irrational. The ethic of nationalism, "my country right or wrong," obscured the fact that the nations were in reality parts of a larger whole and should have been complementary, rather than competitive. Thus the superheated patriotic fervor of the nineteenth century led directly to two world wars in the twentieth. Ironically, these wars led to the redrawing of many frontiers, changing the political allegiance of many of the peoples involved and so invalidating the nationalistic loyalties for which many lives were shed.

Whatever the future of nationalism, and whatever the

basis on which separate national loyalties may eventually be justified, it is now clear that the nation-state cannot claim the ultimate loyalty of any man. We are members of humanity, and the overriding claims of mankind transcend any partial loyalty. But humanity is beyond our grasp; the claims of mankind are ill-defined and unstructured. How can a world of nations be brought into a rational relationship of mutual support and mutual service, and how can the fervor of patriotic zeal be turned to the common good? These are among the unsolved problems for which "applied intellectual power" is needed. But is there a secular answer? Or must the answer rest ultimately in a commitment of faith?

## JAPANESE NATIONALISM

The patriotic fervor that gripped nineteenth century Europe reechoed throughout the world. Japan succeeded, as China did not, in becoming a modern state on the Western model. Japan, being a group of islands, had the advantage of geographical separateness and coherence. It had a strong central government which was able to direct the whole cultural life of the people. In Shinto it had a semireligious, semipatriotic cult which could be used to glorify the nation. Confucian and Buddhist traditions were also strong. Christianity, which had gained a strong following after its first introduction in 1549 but had been suppressed, again became popular after 1868, probably more for what it brought with it than for its essential religious message, though a growing number of Japanese were genuinely converted.

The wars with China (1894-1895) and Russia (1904-1905) launched Japan on a career of military expansion as a highly centralized secular state. Industry and military science followed Western models. The educational system borrowed heavily from Western science and technology, but religion, apart from the "religion of patriotism" (state Shinto), was ignored. After 1920 Japan became a military state, and all areas of life were subordinated to the ambition to dominate the whole of East Asia, if not the whole world. This hope was shattered by defeat in 1945. State Shinto was discredited and abolished. Measures were taken to assure freedom in matters of religion. Buddhism, Christianity and sectarian Shinto shared this freedom together with the "new religions." While the materialistic goals of communism appealed to some, many others sought new spiritual foundations both for personal life and for the nation. More than ever before, Christianity has had a hearing in postwar Japan, though Christians still form a tiny minority of the population.

Japan thus became one of the nations in which religious pluralism is the accepted pattern. Uniting Asian and Western cultural traditions in a unique synthesis, industrially and educationally at the forefront of advance, the Japanese are surely one of the peoples whose influence will count heavily in the choice between secularism and religious faith as the organizing principle of world culture.

## LATIN AMERICAN NATIONALISMS

The republics of Latin America (except Cuba) gained their independence from Spain and Portugal early in the nineteenth century as a delayed consequence of the French Revolution. Simon Bolivar and the other revolutionary leaders believed in liberty, equality and a democratic social order. The liberal movement, however, found itself in con-

flict with the entrenched conservatism of the Roman Catholic Church and the wealthy landowners, while the population included a large proportion of poor, ignorant peasants
and Indians. The result was a protracted struggle, lasting
well into the twentieth century, which was marked by
political instability, social and economic stagnation and
religious futility. Protestantism brought knowledge of the
gospel and personal hope to many who had not found
spiritual sustenance in the Roman Catholic Church. But
the Protestant churches did not have the vision, the social
concern or the influence to deal with the basic evils of
society.

By struggling to maintain its own privileges, the Catholic
Church indirectly strengthened the trend toward secularism.
Liberals sponsored education in lay schools. They advocated separation of church and state and reforms within
the church. The church countered by making common
cause with the great landowners against liberal policies and
progressive ideas. The educated classes found Catholic
thought sterile and turned to materialistic philosophies. The
church lost its earlier concern for the Indians, the peasants,
the poor and the dispossessed.

Following the alliance with the conservatives during the
post-independence period, the hierarchy often regarded social
reform as part of a liberal plot to despoil the Church. Even
in those nations where the Church was secure, the hierarchy
played no role in the quest for social reform. . . . In view of the
profound upheaval in Latin America during the present century,
the loss of identity as the champion of social justice has been
among the most unfortunate consequences for the Church.[3]

Both socially and religiously, therefore, Latin America is
peculiarly vulnerable to the winds of change that are
sweeping over the world today with hurricane force. A

Chilean Jesuit scholar, Father Renato Pablete, states that the advantages of technical civilization are benefiting only a small and select group in Latin America. The great majority have gained nothing but a consciousness of the tremendous contrast between their own situations and what they see they should have.

Social revolution is imminent in many countries of Latin America. The only alternative to violent change is social reconstruction fast enough, deep enough and far-reaching enough to give hope to the hopeless. The churches, Catholic and Protestant, are ill-prepared and ill-equipped to face this prospect. They are desperately understaffed. Their leaders and members are still divided in viewpoint and purpose. Catholics are still too much identified with the wealthy and privileged. Protestants are either too foreign (through identification with North America), too narrowly pietistic, or both. All the churches, and most of the people in them, tend to be conservative and to resist change. Yet there is a forward-looking minority who clearly read the signs of the times and align themselves with the forces of change. It rests with them to make the gospel credible in present-day Latin America.

## THE DEMOCRATIZATION OF SOCIETY

The American and French political revolutions coincided with the early stages of an industrial revolution which is still in process. The goal of the political revolutions was freedom and democracy; but the initial effect of the factory system was a kind of slavery to the machine. The social ferment of the nineteenth and twentieth centuries has sought basically to achieve democratic goals in the industrial field. In a variety of ways churches and religious societies, labor organizations, socialist groups and political parties, governments and the Communist movement have been part of this ferment. All manner of secondary aims, especially that of political domination, have deflected or supplanted the primary goal. The total effect has been an all-pervading and continuing process of change too complex to describe in a few pages. Only its bearing on secularization will be touched on here.

*Democracy*

David Stowe graphically summarizes the bearing of democracy on present-day politics:

Fundamental to politics around the world is the ideology of democracy developed in the West from Biblical and classical roots. The gist of that ideology is an affirmation of dignity and value for every human being regardless of possessions, race, creed or culture, and of his essential equality with everyone else, including an equal right to every advantage which society provides. It means that in some way he shares in the decision-making process, whether through parliamentary democracy or some more subtle means of political participation. It means that all social institutions exist for the benefit of the people, not vice versa—banks, universities, churches, industries, newspapers and all the rest.

No government anywhere can expect to exist on any other premise than this democratic one, however obliquely it may appear to practice its profession. A vivid example is the Chinese government which is widely held to be profoundly undemocratic, yet bases its entire propaganda effort upon the slogan, "*Wei jen-min fu-wu*"—"Serve the people!"

The consequence of this democratic ideology is, almost universally, revolution. In the USA it is the Negro revolution and the revolution of the economically depressed 1/5 of the population. In Britain it is a social-educational revolution. . . . In Latin America it is the ferment which seethes against the privileges of a small elite. Right around the world the revolutionary consequences of democratic ideology can be pointed out.[4]

## *Socialism*

Though Christians have been active in many aspects of social reform, the dominant philosophy of political socialism has been secular and materialistic. As enunciated in the *Communist Manifesto* by Karl Marx and Friedrich Engels in 1848, socialism holds: that the political and intellectual history of any epoch is shaped by the prevailing mode of economic production and exchange; that history is thus a succession of struggles between ruling and oppressed classes; and that emancipating the oppressed entails at the same time "emancipating society at large from all exploitation, oppression, class distinctions and class-struggles."

These precepts make up a platform for the first stages of a social revolution, the stage that sees as its first goal the destruction of privilege. It contains no formula for rebuilding society on a free, classless and nonexploitative basis. Socialists offer no such program. They assert, as a political creed, that by the logic of historical development socialism must be the next stage of social evolution after capitalism, and that the coming society will be better than what has gone before. Not all Socialists advocate violent change. The British Fabians, in particular, believed in progressive, gradual change; and Socialist parties in power have usually been cautious. Furthermore, in advanced nations the diffusion of wealth and advancing standards of social welfare have largely surpassed the original aims of socialism. These advances suggest that the democratic ideal of equal opportunity has gained a large measure of public acceptance, and that the Socialist goal of eliminating class struggle can be reached by nonsocialist roads. By the irony of history it is in backward, rural and underdeveloped areas, rather than in capitalistic countries, that the Socialist ideals have their greatest appeal and face their severest tests.

## Communism

The Russian Socialist party split in 1903 between a moderate minority who trusted in gradual change by peaceful methods and a radical majority who believed in violent revolution. Nikolai Lenin molded the radicals into a tightly knit organization, which was able to seize power in 1917 after the czarist regime collapsed. Lenin and his Communist party tried to apply Marxist teaching in establishing "the dictatorship of the proletariat" as the intermediate stage between capitalism and communism (revolutionary socialism).

Thus a band of revolutionists found themselves suddenly charged with all the responsibilities of governing a badly disorganized nation and administering a complex national economy. They attempted at the same time to transform Russia into a Marxist society without laws, money or private ownership. This attempt led to chaos and economic collapse. A legal code and a monetary system were quickly reintroduced: the incentive value of private profit has been grudgingly recognized. More recently the self-regulation of industry through production for profit has begun to replace bureaucratic planning. Marxism, a theoretical system devised seventy years before the Russian Revolution, simply could not be applied wholesale under modern conditions. Endless modifications have been necessary, and even yet the system is more burdensome, more restrictive and less productive than open societies in which growth and change occur spontaneously.

Like any artificial system, Marxism failed to take account of the rich complexity of human nature with its many interests and drives. It tried to reduce man to an economic equation, and even at that level it misread some of the facts. For instance, it uprooted the highly productive system of privately owned farms, replacing them with huge collective farms run like factories. In so doing it encountered fierce resistance from the peasants, who loved their land. Many slaughtered their livestock rather than turn it over to the collective farms. Reduced to the level of anonymous workers, without initiative or incentive, the people worked poorly. Output declined catastrophically. Concessions had to be made, especially in permitting each farm family a private garden plot. But the collective system still burdens the nation's economy.

Communism has been notoriously unsuccessful in agriculture, both in Russia and in China. But in every field communism undervalued personal initiative and creativity. Regimentation is a poor substitute for spontaneity and freedom. Slogans lose their glamor. Propaganda ceases to persuade. The creed of Marxist orthodoxy is repeated with less and less conviction until it becomes mere words. So the sacrificial commitment with which great numbers of young people responded to communism as to a new faith, first in Russia and later in China, has in many cases worn thin with the passage of time. But long after that happens the system remains unshaken, because in the meantime it has entrenched itself in power.

Marxist doctrine is not merely secular, that is, unconcerned with religion—it is actively antireligious. Marx and Lenin saw religion only as an element in the structure of privilege and power they sought to overthrow. They held that the churches helped the rulers keep the people in subjection by substituting future hope for present gain. No doubt there was an element of truth in this judgment. But they missed the deeper reality. Personal faith as a genuine source of courage, character and motivation was beyond their understanding. So they held that religion was an enemy to be destroyed. Whereas the political state could be left to wither away, religion was a perversion that must be combatted by actively teaching atheism. But the hold of religion was deeper than the Communist leaders supposed. Popular faith has survived and helped the people to survive. During World War II the Russian authorities even sought the help of the churches in their efforts to bolster the nation's morale. Churches and theological schools were permitted to reopen. "Spiritual interests" are sharply demarcated from the political and economic functions of the state, but as long as this distinction is observed religious activities often remain unmolested. Yet atheism is still the official dogma of communism, and antireligious indoctrination continues.

Theoretical Marxism had little interest in politics, but Soviet Russia turned to political action as a primary means of communizing the world. Bolshevik leaders expected that the Russian Revolution of 1917 would touch off similar explosions everywhere. Disappointed, they settled down to a slow process of indoctrination and subversion, taking advantage of every situation of social unrest or instability. China was a particular target, and the Chinese Nationalist movement was thoroughly infiltrated with Communist agents. The tactics there and elsewhere were to foment discontent and provoke civil strife, so that orderly government would become impossible until Communist leaders were put in control. Once in power they could apply dictatorial methods to suppress opposition and restore order, thus "proving" the superiority of communism. The Japanese invasion of China was the final weakening factor that opened the way for a complete Communist take-over.

In Europe Communist activity provoked the rise of fascism as a counterforce. World War II was the outcome. After the war Soviet leaders again expected communism to prevail throughout Europe. The satellite states of Central Europe total a much smaller territorial gain than they had hoped for, and are at present less securely held in the Communist orbit than they could wish. Communism as a mode of national organization does not possess the inherent advantages claimed for it; and in this respect it is a waning force. The polarization of the world into Communist and anti-Communist blocs is a temporary situation. Meanwhile the emergence of China as a Communist power strong enough to challenge Russian leadership of the Communist forces has thrown the whole movement into disarray and created a new element of uncertainty.

## POST-COLONIAL NATION BUILDING

After World War I the Treaty of Versailles recognized the right of national self-determination, but it gave no clue to how small a people could claim to be a nation, or how several intermingled peoples sharing the same territory could unscramble themselves. The treaty makers were thinking chiefly of Europe, and it did not immediately occur to them that the peoples under colonial rule could also lay claim to the right of self-determination. But it did very soon occur to the peoples involved. First in Asia and then in Africa, movements to end colonial rule began to gather

strength. India was the first and the most populous nation
to gain its independence—an event unhappily marred by
the partitioning off of Pakistan and the mass displacement
of millions of people, Hindus in one direction and Muslims
in the other, with untold suffering on both sides.

There is no doubt that the liberation movements expressed the genuine aspirations of the peoples concerned.
Self-rule would have come anyway, and rightly, but there is
no doubt either that the movement was hastened by
East-West tensions and rivalries. Liberation of the downtrodden is the first principle of Marxism, and the Communists naturally regarded themselves as the champions of
subject peoples—often to the embarrassment of the peoples
concerned. They tried, as always, to exploit every conflict
to their own ends, and to make every anti-colonial movement into a Communist revolution. Again their success was
limited and fleeting. No people that has managed to throw
off one yoke of subjection will knowingly accept another.
The ranks of neutral, unaligned young nations have steadily
grown; the ranks of Communist states have not experienced
a corresponding increase.

But speeding up the process of decolonization has meant
that many young nations have become self-governing suddenly, without any period of transition and with no ap-
prenticeship in politics or administration. They have not
had time to discover their own most gifted leaders, to take
the measure of the problems confronting them, to form a
consensus on policy or even, in some cases, to begin to
think of themselves as a nation. It needs no prophet to
foresee that a period of uncertainty lies ahead. Every possible resource of integrity, decisiveness of character and
devotion to the public good will be needed. Will the faith

orientation of national leaders and of the people generally make a difference? Surely it should.

In the new nations, numberless people at all levels of society and in all manner of responsible positions will make decisions involving others besides themselves. By education, training and administrative control the technical competence of persons for the work they do can be reasonably well assured. But the healthy functioning of society requires more than competence. An overseas correspondent writes of the need for more "dedicated men and women who are eager to serve and less afraid of doing something a bit irregular than of doing nothing at all except holding down a post." It is this *élan,* this surplus of dedication, initiative, courage and purpose that will often make the difference between achievement and failure. It is here that faith—commitment to an ultimate beyond oneself—provides a power that transcends the rational calculations of secularism.

## MARXISM, SOCIAL AWARENESS AND THE CHURCHES

Even this brief review of the emergent secularism of the past century raises questions: Why has Marxist doctrine exerted such profound and far-reaching influence throughout the world? Why does it continue to do so? What is its significance as a secular alternative to religious faith?

Clearly the answer does not lie in the correctness or adequacy of its social theory, for it neither fits all the facts nor works well in practice. Still less does the answer lie in its antireligious bias, which was based on a total misconstruction of what religious faith is and does.

Marxism is significant because it has turned the light of rational inquiry on the class structure of society and the causes of poverty. It has challenged the assumption that privilege and status were preordained and not subject to question. It has opened the whole field of social justice to analysis, and so to corrective action. It has done this publicly, lifting up these new ideas as a bright new hope for the poor. Thus it has become a major secularizing force. Its message has been: "You are not bound by nature or by fate to suffer oppression or injustice. Evils can be remedied. Rise up and free yourselves."

As a message to mankind, Marxism was prophetic and timely. Increasingly the shape of society is subject to human control. Inequities and social evils *can* be corrected, and therefore it becomes a duty to learn how to correct them and to do what is needed. Marxism is a continuing challenge to work incessantly at social renewal as an obligation of the highest urgency.

By casting the doctrine in the form of a message *for* the poor and *against* the rich, the pioneers of socialism set the stage for class conflict and revolutionary struggle. This is not the ideal way to achieve change. Study, mutual understanding, negotiation and amicable settlement are more rational, but the holders of power are often deaf to any appeal but that of force. The pent-up passion of the exploited is a kind of social dynamite that sometimes serves a necessary purpose; though, once unleashed, it may destroy the very fabric of society. Modern man will not be wholly master of his situation until he learns to anticipate grievances and correct wrongs before they fester.

For the churches, the field of corrective social action opened up by Marxism was a totally new domain. The churches had been thinking microscopically—in terms of individuals, families and parishes. Socialism studied society in national or even world terms and proposed mass action on the whole structure of society. There is nothing reprehensible in the fact that few Christian leaders in the mid-nineteenth century grasped the significance of the new movement or gave it support. Few non-Christians did either. But it would be reprehensible to remain unconcerned now. Christians are answerable before God if when faced with a challenge to act in a good cause they content themselves with words, or worse still, stand aside and do nothing. Social justice and social reform on many fronts *are* good causes, and the reluctance of many Christians to involve themselves in "controversial matters" is explainable in only one of two ways: they do not yet understand where their duty lies—in which case they must learn—or they are afraid.

In this respect Communists, with their total commitment to the renewal of society, often put Christians to shame. Tracey K. Jones tells how Christians in Communist China have been humbled:

. . . To their surprise Christians found themselves dealing with Communist leaders, most of them young, who were hard workers, disciplined, and self-confident. Christians soon realized that the Communists were ready to sacrifice themselves for their cause with an abandon that Christians did not feel towards theirs. They also discovered that there was an unexpected puritanical strain in the Communists. Prostitution was stamped out. The subtle forms of political corruption that had undermined so much Chinese political life were brought under control. It was a shock to the Christian to find that the Communists did what Christians had for so long claimed to be their objective. In the new Communist society it was the lower classes, the workers, the peasants, the underprivileged, who were elevated to the highest position of prestige. As we see now, much of this was a hoax. Yet it is true that a new relationship has been established between the scholar and the ordinary worker. . . . Christians have been humbled by their realization in years past that they did not identify themselves as they should have with the common people.[5]

This situation brings to mind Jesus' story:

. . . A man had two sons. He went to the first, and said, "My boy, go and work today in the vineyard." "I will, sir," the boy replied; but he never went. The father came to the second and said the same. "I will not," he replied, but afterwards he changed his mind and went. (Matthew 21:28-30, NEB)

The purposes of God are better served by those who work for righteousness without professing obedience than by those who profess without working. The stance of Christians and of churches in the revolutionary changes yet to come will be critical *for the church,* but not decisive for the purpose of God. For the church is but an instrument in his hands; his purpose relates to the whole world.

## SECULARIZATION: SETTING FOR GOD'S ACTION

The sequence we have been tracing marks the increasing ability of man to shape and control society, as he had earlier learned to dominate nature. Expanding and advancing technology makes this second stage possible. Every step along this road increases man's power to make decisions that will shape the future of the race. Not *all* men—for most are still relatively humble and unburdened with responsibility—but *some* men have to decide how these new powers will be used. Powers that were formerly in God's hands are passing into the hands of men.

Some see in this situation the triumph of man over God. "Man is in fact the measure of all things," they say. "The whole universe is within his grasp." Some would go further and say that God has abdicated. He has left the world in men's hands and is no longer active in its affairs. Then it is only a short step to the final negation: "God never was in the world. Man has to cope with it alone. There might as well not be a God. *Perhaps there is none!*"

Agnostic secularism takes this position, and thus reduces God to the measure of man's mind. Certainly the bourgeois God against whom Marx rebelled is dead. He never existed. He has gone the way of the gods of rocks and trees, of sacred graves and temples, of separate tribes and nations. Gods *within creation* belong to the childhood of man. "When I became a man, I gave up childish ways." So adult man must say farewell to his childish imaginings about God. In the spiritual as well as the physical realm, man must grow up.

Even the secularist, however, depends on the regularity of nature. The consistent operation of natural law is the very foundation of man's dominion over nature. In the same way social control rests, as it has since the days of Confucius, on "a natural order which is also a moral order." Social justice has meaning only within such a frame of reference—written in the heart of man, implicit in his nature as man. The stream of events becomes history only when it is seen as an ordered sequence in which result follows cause and the effects of human choices can be traced. Intelligent, purposeful, responsible human action would be impossible without these dependable regularities. They do not preclude human freedom; they make it possible.

Christians hold that the entire cosmic order is the work of God and bears witness to God. The prologue to the Gospel according to John declares this explicitly. As clearly as words can state the ultimate mystery it declares that the *Word,* the active principle of order that underlies all creation, was God's self-expression.

At the beginning God expressed himself. That personal expression, that word, was with God and was God, and he existed with God from the beginning. All creation took place through him, and none took place without him. In him appeared life and this life was the light of mankind. The light still shines in the darkness, and the darkness has never put it out. (John 1:1-5)[6]

Secularization does not negate God's action in history. Rather it justifies the affirmation that a new stage is at hand in the working out of God's purpose for man—that man shall attain a stature of mature, responsible selfhood beyond anything he has yet reached. This too is in accordance with Christian faith. St. Paul spoke of the hidden wisdom of God,

his secret purpose framed from the very beginning to bring us to our full glory . . . in the words of Scripture, "Things beyond our seeing, things beyond our hearing, things beyond our imagining, all prepared by God for those who love him," these it is that God has revealed to us through the spirit.
For the spirit explores everything, even the depths of God's own nature. (1 Cor. 2:7, 9-10, NEB)

The increase of human powers is an irreversible process, in which each step entails a new weight of responsibility. Knowledge once acquired becomes part of the heritage of the race, which could be totally lost only through the destruction of civilization. But the wisdom to use knowledge beneficially is not conferred by nature. It is the responsibility of men to learn wisdom, so that knowledge will benefit mankind.

Increasing powers, which enhance freedom in one direction, restrict it in another. Nations that have atomic weapons in their arsenals are less free to engage in reckless military adventures than they were when they did not have them. Drivers of high-powered automobiles in heavy traffic have to be more safety-conscious as well as more skillful than their grandfathers who drove Model-T Fords.

As a consequence of current research, discovery and achievement in a number of scientific fields, no ideas about future transformations in the lives of men seem too wild to contemplate. In sober scientific circles today there is hardly a subject more commonly discussed than man's control of his own heredity and evolution. And the discussions seldom leave much doubt that man will acquire this control. It is a matter of *when,* not if. All of which means that brain-cracking complexities—legal, social, ethical, moral, philosophical, religious—are soon to be thrust upon us.[7]

Once again scientific and technological advance raises issues that transcend the secular realm. Only within the ultimate frame of reference in which religious faith moves can men deal with them.

# 5 Beyond Religion: God in Christ

     WHEN JESUS TALKED WITH THE WOMAN OF Samaria she tried to move the discussion onto safe, impersonal ground by asking a question about religion.

> . . . "Sir," she replied, "I can see that you are a prophet. Our fathers worshipped on this mountain, but you Jews say that the temple where God should be worshipped is in Jerusalem." [But Jesus transposed the issue from the level of religion to the deeper realm of faith.] "Believe me," said Jesus, . . . "the time approaches, indeed it is already here, when those who are real worshippers will worship the Father in spirit and in truth. Such are the worshippers whom the Father wants." (John 4:19-24, NEB)

Throughout the preceding chapters this distinction between religion and faith has been reiterated. No one has *seen* God at any time, but every people has apprehended his presence and responded to it. The outward forms of those responses are the religions of mankind. They involve temples and rituals, myths and commandments, sacred places and persons and books, doctrines and theological systems. Diverse as they are in form and content, all religions are prompted by faith. The source of that faith is God—the God who seeks, always and everywhere, for those who will worship him "in spirit and in truth."

Paradoxical though it may seem, even the Marxist who

professes atheism is moved by the same spirit, because it is his righteous passion for social justice that drives him to denounce a God whom he identifies with the sins of the complacent, exploiting class of society. This is an instance of the recurrent fact that the emphases, including distortions and false emphases, of any religion are the result of historical circumstances interacting with personal faith. They reflect the strivings of men and women in a particular time and place and culture. It is necessary to do as Max Warren once suggested:

Our task is to ask what is the authentic religious content of the experience of the Hindu when he seeks to identify himself with Bramah, of the Buddhist when he seeks to escape from desire, of the Muslim when he submits to the will of Allah. We may rightly conclude that in their analysis of Reality the Hindu, the Buddhist, and the Muslim have started from a false premise and reached a faulty conclusion. But we must not reach that conclusion by arguing from outside their religious situation. We have to try to sit where they sit, to enter sympathetically into the pains and griefs and joys of their history and see how those pains and griefs and joys have determined the premises of their argument, and then to make the leap of faith by which we recognize that the love of God has embraced them also, that they have responded authentically to that love, and that at the point of their authenticity and our authenticity we can meet and speak to each other in the presence of God.[1]

In meeting "at the point of authenticity," we must recognize that we too are conditioned by our past. Like other religions the Christian religion as we know it is the cumulative result of "the pains and griefs and joys" of past generations of Christians and of the conflicts and cultures that shaped them, while at the same time it embodies one stream of authentic response to the self-revelation of God. In fact the particular Christianity we happen to know best is one of a number of Christianities, which differ so widely that they appear to be different religions. To the casual observer a silent Quaker meeting would seem to have nothing in common with a Roman Catholic high mass. The Presbyterian emphasis on doctrine seems unrelated to the holy mysteries of the Eastern Orthodox liturgies. Twenty centuries of church history have overlaid the gospel of Jesus Christ and the authentic faith response of his followers with much that is secondary or obsolete. Even matters of central importance have to be restated from generation to generation because thought forms and concepts and modes of expression change. Even the Bible must frequently be retranslated so that it speaks in today's idiom.

In *Challenge and Response,* Max Warren asks why the number of converts to Christianity in Asia has been small in proportion to the whole population. By and large, he says, Asians, and especially Asian leaders of great stature, have rejected the Christianity with which they have had contact. The reason is threefold:

> . . . Christianity has been rejected for its Westernness, its arrogance, and its irrelevance. For such men Christianity is a symbol of a long-maintained cultural attack on the integrity of Asia's own socio-religious life, of an attempt to provide a religious support to political aggression, of a failure to offer Asia a basis for its own reconstruction. Christianity so far has *felt* foreign.[2]

We are therefore under the necessity of discovering that point of authenticity at the heart of Christianity which is *not* Western but universal, which is *not* arrogant but self-giving, and which is *not* irrelevant but central to the nature and needs of all men at the deepest level of their being.

This point of authenticity is Jesus Christ, as he is made known in the gospels and reflected in the other books of the New Testament. He must speak and we must listen. We must learn not to obtrude our interpretations of him or our traditions about him. For what he says today, to others and to us, may not be what we expect him to say, but something quite different. We must learn to see him through Asian and African eyes—and through the skeptical eyes of secularists as well. We must discern what he says that matters to them, because his word to them is also his word to us through them. And so the barriers of arrogance and hostility and misunderstanding between them and us will fall.

Are we in such doubt of the truth of the surpassing glory revealed in the face of Jesus Christ that we are afraid of such an encounter with a non-Christian, skeptical of the converting power of the Christ whom both of us meet at this point of meeting? Can we be ready to learn from the other man and so become to him an interpreter of the Christ we know? . . .

Asia is challenging us by its repudiation of and revulsion from much that has been all too common in the traditional missionary approach to the non-Christian religions. I believe that the challenge, for all its vigor and sometimes violence, is at least wistful. There are many in Asia today who are coming to Christians and saying . . . "Sirs, we would see Jesus."[3]

## THE FAITH OF JESUS

### Heritage

Jesus stands at the parting of the ways between Judaism and Christianity. First century Judaism was a national religion, based in the covenant relation between Israel and Israel's God which was the central fact of Jewish history and the focus of Jewish national identity. But the God whom the people of Israel worshiped was more than a national deity, he was the supreme God, Creator of the world, Ruler and Judge of all mankind, whose purpose was—and is—

working itself out in all history. The knowledge and worship of this God, the true and only God, "whose majesty fills the earth" could not remain permanently the private possession of one small nation. Jewish prophets had declared that it was God's purpose that Israel should be a light to the nations. Long before the prophets, according to the Jewish tradition, God had promised the patriarch Abraham, . . . "by your descendants shall all the nations of the earth bless themselves, because you have obeyed my voice." (Gen. 22:18)

It was in and through Jesus Christ that this universal faith broke out of the restricting confines of Jewish nationalism into the broad stream of world history. Our knowledge of that event is contained in the books of the New Testament, records largely contemporary with the event itself. It is clear from the New Testament that the message proclaimed by Paul and his fellow missionaries in the Mediterranean world was already somewhat different in content from Jesus' own teaching. In fact, Paul's thought centers in Christ the risen Lord, whom he had first encountered on the road to Damascus and whose continuing unseen presence was the basic conviction of his faith. Paul rarely refers to the earthly ministry or teaching of Jesus. Probably they never met in the flesh.

But it is Jesus, not Paul, who is the pioneer of our faith. It is therefore fortunate that in the gospels we have records of "all that Jesus began to do and to teach." Without the gospels Jesus would be to us only a figure of legend devoid of human content. Through them we are able, in a sense, to sit at his feet and hear him teach, much as his disciples did nearly two thousand years ago. His own faith speaks through his words and actions. So we are permitted to share his awareness of God and to enter into the relationship to God that he offered—and still offers—to his disciples.

Of course the gospels are not biography in the modern sense. They make no claim to provide a "life of Jesus Christ." They are recollections of what he did and said, colored by reflection and by a growing realization of his transcendent stature. They are written out of the context of faith and seek to declare the source of that faith.

> . . . there are no analogies to the message of Jesus. There is no parallel to his message that God is concerned with sinners and not with the righteous, and that he grants them, here and now, a share in his kingdom. There is no parallel to Jesus' sitting down in table-fellowship with publicans and sinners . . . [nor] to the authority with which he dares to address God as *abba* [father]. . . . That is the fact to which the sources bear witness: a man appeared, and those who received his message were certain that they had heard the word of God.[4]

He speaks, of course, in the idiom of first century Palestine. Jesus was a Jew. So were his hearers. They shared the religious heritage of their nation, which is known to us through the Old Testament and other records. It is known to us, so to speak, from the outside; we do not and we cannot share the depth of feeling with which they cried "we are Abraham's children," or the passion of their longing for the liberation of Israel and the coming of the promised kingdom. Yet that very intensity of concern imprisoned them in the nationalistic religion of Judaism. They were so bound by it that *by themselves* they could neither see nor grasp the universal implications of their faith. The supreme genius of Jesus is seen in the fact that from within the Jewish tradition he was able to affirm his faith in terms that remain valid for all men and for all time. Thus those who heard and responded became a liberated fellowship, the leaven of a new community taking form within the old community.

## Discipleship

The response that Jesus sought was not intellectual assent to propositions *about* God, but the *decision to serve God* in active discipleship. "Disciple" means "learner," but Jesus said in effect: "To learn more of God's will, do the good you already know. Do not wait to reason out principles. Do not try to see the end from the beginning. God loves you. Trust him, respond to his love, and you will begin to know what you ought to do to serve him. And then keep on, step by step." Thus for Jesus, discipleship is consistency in making life's decisions on the basis of commitment, love, goodwill and concern for others. Knowledge and wisdom, judgment and experience contribute to right decision making, of course; they are not ends in themselves. They are servants of the will in making the whole person "a doer of the word, and not a hearer only."

We know, of course, that complete consistency in living on the basis of love, goodwill and concern for others is never attainable. We fail not only because courage falters and the flesh is weak, but because we never see things in their true light. Selfishness is always present. Reinhold Niebuhr points out that man is not the harmless individual activated only by desire to survive which secular idealism has assumed him to be. Animals are moved by an instinctive desire to survive, but man wants more.

. . . Man is the kind of animal who cannot merely live. If he lives at all he is bound to seek the realization of his true nature; and to his true nature belongs his fulfillment in the lives of others . . . self-realization involves self-giving in relations to others. . . . Thus the will-to-live is finally transmuted into its opposite . . . for: "He that findeth his life shall lose it, and he that loseth his life for my sake shall find it." (Matt. 10:39)

On the other hand the will-to-live is also spiritually transmuted into . . . the desire for "power and glory." Man . . . is not interested merely in physical survival but in prestige and social approval. . . . [He] invariably seeks to gain security . . . by enhancing his power, individually and collectively. . . . [He] seeks to compensate for his insignificance by pretensions of pride. . . .

[Hence] man is at variance with himself. . . . The fact that the two impulses . . . are also mixed and compounded with each other on every level of human life, makes the simple distinctions between good and evil, between selfishness and altruism, with which liberal idealism has tried to estimate moral and political facts, invalid. The fact that the will-to-power inevitably justifies itself in terms of the morally more acceptable will to realize man's true nature means that the egoistic corruption of universal ideals is a much more persistent fact in human conduct than any moralistic creed is inclined to admit.[5]

Thus the Christian disciple always lives in tension between the two forces in his nature. But he accepts this tension as the mark of discipleship, symbolized for Christians in the cross, and actualized in the harsh daily discipline of deciding for "the hard right as against the easy wrong."

Superficial critics charge that the way of Christ is impracticable because it is never fully attainable. But that is precisely its value. Wherever a man stands, the directional arrow of discipleship still points beyond him. Any set of rules would become outmoded. They would be too hard for some, too easy for others; and changing situations would make them irrelevant. But Jesus did not propose rules. To love others *as* one loves oneself is an inexhaustible standard of action and of relationships, which everyone can apply in his own situation. Love of neighbor, which is the expression and consequence of trust in God, both strengthens the will and subjects one's motives to the searching light of a transcendent standard. "Only God is good," said Jesus. No man can claim credit before him or acquire merit in his sight. It is not that we are completely bad, but that our self-giving is never complete, never finished.

> Suppose one of you has a servant ploughing or minding sheep. When he comes back from the fields, will the master say, "Come along at once and sit down"? Will he not rather say, "Prepare my supper, buckle your belt, and then wait on me while I have my meal; you can have yours afterwards"? Is he grateful to the servant for carrying out his orders? So with you: when you have carried out all your orders, you should say, "We are servants and deserve no credit; we have only done our duty." (Luke 17:7-10, NEB)

## The Content of Obedience

Jesus' hearers had a ready-made standard of obedience in the law, which was ascribed by tradition to Moses but was actually a compendium from many epochs and sources. In part it was the social and moral code of the nation, in part the ritual code of worship, purification and sacrifice. It had become excessively burdensome, largely because legalists kept expanding it to provide specific guidance for every conceivable situation. Religious leaders taught that meticulous observance of the law was pleasing to God. In theory all points were equally binding. In practice, however, value judgments were brought to bear. Three of the gospels record a discussion between Jesus and a lawyer as to which law was the most important. Though the stories varied, the answer was the same in each case: Ethical demands are "weightier matters" than tithing herbs. To love God and neighbor were the primary commandments.

But Jesus dealt more radically with the law than other teachers had done: ". . . he taught as one who had authority." He went behind the formal prohibitions of murder, adultery, false witness and revenge to the basic questions of motive and relationships which give rise to evil acts. He did not hesitate to disregard ritual requirements as immaterial, or to redefine "defilement" in terms of malicious acts rather than unclean food. He declared that the Sabbath was made for man, and not the other way round, and thereby reduced the status of all cultic observances. He brought moral and ritual requirements out of the inscrutable realm of the holy and made them subject to the practical judgment of usefulness and common sense. For he clearly believed that God has endowed men with the power of moral judgment and expects them to use it. Time after time, when people brought questions to him he turned the questions back and asked them how they judged the issue.

Thus he liberated men from subjection to arbitrary, externally imposed moral and religious law. He carried to fulfillment the prophetic word of Jeremiah: "I will put my law within them, and I will write it in their hearts; and I will be their God and they shall be my people." (Jer. 31:33)

In this connection Rudolf Bultmann quotes Jesus' words:

> "Take my yoke upon you and learn from me . . .
>
> For my yoke is easy,
>
> and my burden is light."

He comments:

The obedience for which Jesus asks is easy, because it frees a man from dependence on a formal authority, and therefore frees him also from the judgment of the men whose profession it is to explain this authority. Such obedience is easy, because it

depends on the judgment and responsibility of the one concerned. Of course from another angle it is all the more difficult.
For to the weak man it is a relief to have the judgment of good
and evil and all *responsibility* taken away from him. And *this*
burden is just what Jesus puts upon men; he teaches men to
see themselves as called to *decision*—decision between good and
evil, decision for God's will or for their own will.[6]

We should, however, recall that Jesus generally had in
mind the collective judgment and obedience of the whole
fellowship, or at least of a group large enough to sustain
one another, rather than that of the individual by himself.
He sent his followers on mission two by two, not one by
one. He promised the disciples that where two or three
of them were gathered together "in his name"—with a
common commitment to him—he would "be among them,"
and again that "if two of you agree on earth about anything they ask, it will be done for them by my Father in
heaven." And yet again, in words that seem strange to us:
. . . "whatever you bind on earth shall be bound in heaven,
and whatever you loose on earth shall be loosed in heaven."
(Matt. 18:19, 18) If men make social and moral judgments with integrity of commitment to God and concern
for others, those judgments carry their own authority; God
has vested in men the right and the competence to make
responsible judgments and will not override them. And,
so far as possible, the weakness and self-will of the individual is corrected by the common judgment and united
commitment of the fellowship. *God's free people are an
instrument through which he works in history.*

## The Kingdom of God

It is clear from the gospels that both Jesus and his hearers
expected a sudden, dramatic end to the existing order of

things, to be followed by a miraculous new age. According to the popular hope Israel was to be delivered from bondage and reestablished as a kingdom ruled by a son of David—perhaps a supernatural figure sent from heaven. Some predicted that the dead would rise and undergo judgment, that the scattered tribes of Israel would return to swell the nation and that all the nations on the earth would stand in awe of the glory of Israel.

Jesus never contradicted these hopes, but neither did he encourage them. He seems to have taken figuratively rather than literally the highly colored language in which they were expressed. He made no prediction about the time or manner in which God would fulfill his purpose, disclaimed any special knowledge about it and cautioned his disciples against fruitless speculation. Whatever might happen, it would be God's doing, not man's. No one, Jew or Gentile, could claim a place in the kingdom as a matter of right, but only as God's gift. The kingdom, in his eyes, was certainly not a new social order of man's making. Biblical scholars are right in pointing out that any idea of "building the kingdom of God on earth" is foreign to the teaching of Jesus—as is the transference of the kingdom to life after death or to the end of history.

But one wonders if scholars in wrestling with the riddles of "the end of the age" have not tended to overlook the obvious. Most of Jesus' teaching about the kingdom has no obvious reference to the *messianic* kingdom at all. Some of the parables mention the kingdom of God; others do not, but they all describe *the way God's rule operates—the shape of the real, viable world of human relationships that he is bringing into being.* Jesus seems to have taken the popular messianic expectation as a peg on which to hang new truth; but that new truth is valid in its own right, independently of any fulfillment of the messianic hope. It is in fact nonhistorical in the same way that the law of gravitation is nonhistorical—it is not more valid at one place or time than another. It is not conditioned by any specific event.

Perhaps the lack of obvious reference to the messianic hope in many of the parables accounts for the mystification they caused his hearers. People did not hear what they expected to hear, and so they did not really hear after all. But the stories were vivid and pithy, and they stuck in the mind. They served—and still serve—their intended purpose, that of sharpening the call to decision for or against the intention of God at every point in the life of any hearer. The Jewish messianic hope became in Jesus a summons to know God and to obey him. And this hope is not limited to one time or one people, but is open to all mankind.

## Forgiveness, Reconciliation and Healing

Forgiveness is a central concern in the faith and teaching of Jesus. Within the brief compass of the Lord's Prayer stands the petition, "Forgive us our debts as we forgive our debtors." Reconciliation, said Jesus, has priority even over worship. "So if you are offering your gift at the altar, and there remember that your brother has something against you, leave your gift there before the altar and go; first be reconciled to your brother, and then come and offer your gift." (Matt. 5:23-24) The implication is clear: A person who is unable to forgive or to seek reconciliation cannot receive forgiveness. The same point is made in several parables, and in some very emphatic teachings: Forgive not seven times only, but seventy times seven. Turn the other cheek. Go the second mile. Here again Jesus was restoring to man a responsibility which the legalists had reserved to God. "Who can forgive sins but God alone?" (Mark 2:7) Thus he freed men from dependence on the religious authorities who administered rites of absolution and purification.

But he was also charging men with a duty and privilege toward one another which had never before been spelled out so clearly. In the course of time Paul gave it a name: *the ministry of reconciliation.* Writing with the exuberant joy that always filled him when he thought of Christ, Paul exclaimed, "Therefore, if anyone is in Christ, he is a new creation; the old has passed away, behold, the new has come. All this is from God, who through Christ reconciled us to himself and gave us the ministry of reconciliation. . . ." (2 Cor. 5:17-18)

This is a much more emphatic cry of liberation than we might expect, even from Paul. For it is here that Jesus most decisively reversed the prevailing assumptions about God and so declared the new relationship, which he afterward sealed with his own life. Only those who have gone through a profound experience of estrangement, forgiveness and reconciliation will know how completely everything is changed by it. And here it is not a matter of reconciliation among men, but of man's relation to God.

The basic assumption, not only of Judaism but of mankind generally, has been that retribution serves the cause of justice. "An eye for an eye, and a tooth for a tooth" is instinctive morality. Let the punishment fit the crime, but if anything, err on the side of severity as a warning to others. Throughout history this has been an axiom of human relations. But as a social principle retributive justice leads straight to disaster, for it easily becomes vindictive. It tends to exact great penalties for small faults, exploits human frailty and gives moral support to the desire for power. In ancient Israel, therefore, the principle of retribution had already been supplemented by the law of jubilee, which provided for periodic clearing of old accounts and the release of persons bound over for debt. Justice was tempered with mercy, but the principle of retribution remained unchallenged.

The same principle was believed to hold between man and God, but even more stringently, because the whole moral order of the world was assumed to rest on the unswerving justice of God. The Jewish faith in the moral purity of God was certainly a great advance over the unmoral gods of the heathen peoples around them, but it was only a first step. Jesus took the second step in declaring that God is not bound by his own righteousness. He is not vindictive but merciful by nature. He pours the bounty of his creation on all his creatures, whether they love and honor him or not. The whole world is his, for he made it. We are his possession, and we can never buy ourselves free no matter how hard we try. The whole idea of earning his favor by sacrifice or merit is ruled out; and the only honest position a man can take toward God is boundless gratitude for life and all its blessings and contrition for misusing them.

Does God's compassionate love mean that he does not judge men at all? Not in the least. It means that the basis of his judgment is whether a man repays God's goodness to him by his own goodness to other people. Recall Jesus' story of the king who settled accounts with his servants (Matt. 18:23-35). One man owed him millions which he could not pay, and the master forgave him. But the same man threw a fellow-servant into jail for a paltry debt. So the king called him and said: ". . . were you not bound to show your fellow-servant the same pity as I showed to you?" Then he condemned him to torture until he paid the whole debt. "And that," said Jesus, "is how my heavenly Father will deal with you, unless you each forgive your brother from your hearts." (NEB)

The new covenant in Christ is a covenant of forgiveness (see Matt. 26:28). The petition "Forgive us our debts as we forgive our debtors" is a perpetual reminder of that covenant and a call to self-examination. Thus committed trust in the forgiving love of God becomes the fountainhead of an overflowing stream of positive goodwill toward men.

An individual's *ability to receive* God's liberating grace depends on his willingness to forgive and to be reconciled wherever there has been enmity. Unless we truly forgive others we cannot know forgiveness. Those who are "in Christ," as Paul says, and who therefore know at first hand the "new creation" of reconciliation with God, are charged with the ministry of reconciliation. As a result, they are not merely passive bystanders but are motivated to become directly involved wherever a helping or moderating or conciliating presence is needed. The healers of rifts, the peacemakers, the merciful, the bearers of other people's burdens—these are among the ministers of reconciliation. And their ministry brings them face to face with the harsh realities of human self-centeredness (often cloaked under the appearance of virtue).

Reconciliation means bringing two sides together in mutual trust and collaboration. One cannot urge the downtrodden to forgive their exploiters without also trying to make the exploiters aware of the obligation to take every possible step to correct the evils they are causing. Ministers of reconciliation—in the Christian sense—are able to face the reality of evil, in themselves and in others, without subterfuge or excuse, because they know forgiveness is there, waiting to be grasped. Repentance, change of heart, forgiving and being forgiven; these are not empty words. They describe what happens when one takes seriously Jesus' word of forgiveness and reconciliation.

The field of action of Christian reconciliation is *the world*. It is not contained within the walls of the church or restricted to members of the Christian fellowship. It is not sacral (church-administered) but social in the most inclusive sense. Yet it is sacramental, for the act of sincere forgiveness between persons is the "outward and visible sign of an inward and spiritual grace," namely a chastened spirit newly opened to reconciliation and love. This is, in Bonhoeffer's phrase, "religionless Christianity."

For the word has been spoken to all mankind. *Authentic* faith penetrates beyond the veil of a particular tradition to the ultimate reality which is God. Jesus Christ says that God is reconciling love. When men trust that love they confirm its reality and power. Is this the "point of authenticity" of faith to which everything else is secondary? If so, we must be careful how we use the term "*Christian* reconciliation." It is Christian in the sense that it comes to us through the faith of Jesus Christ and in his person. It is Christian in the sense that it presupposes the merciful God whom he called Father, and that the covenant of forgiveness is a prayer to that God as "*Our* Father." It is Christian in the sense that the community of Christians should be—and partly is—a reconciled and reconciling fellowship. But the fellowship is wider than the church, and the churches as institutions bearing the name "Christian" have no proprietary claim over the reconciling action of God. The use of the word "Christian" must not become a barrier to the free action of God's grace outside the church as well as inside.

### THE PERSON OF CHRIST

Jesus fulfilled in his own life the obedience to which he called mankind. In him the shadowy figure of "the suffering servant" (Isaiah 40-55) became a historic reality. He defined his ministry, in words quoted from Isaiah, as that of a herald sent from God with a message of liberation.

> The Spirit of the Lord is upon me,
> because he has anointed me to preach good news
>     to the poor.
> He has sent me to proclaim release to the
>     captives
> and recovering of sight to the blind,
> to set at liberty those who are oppressed,
> to proclaim the acceptable year of the Lord.
>                 (Luke 4:18-19 cf. Isaiah 61:1-2)

He sought no status for himself other than that of servant to God and man. He allowed others to make up their minds about him on the basis of what they saw and heard: "Who do men say that I am? . . . and who do *you* say?"

He enjoined his disciples not to seek rank or authority.

"You know that those who are supposed to rule over the Gentiles lord it over them, and their great men exercise authority over them. But it shall not be so among you; but whoever would be great among you must be your servant, and whoever would be first among you must be slave of all. For the Son of man also came not to be served but to serve, and to give his life as a ransom for many." (Mark 10:42-45)

The washing of the disciples' feet at the Last Supper—a menial task—was symbolic, but utterly without pretense for it was fully in keeping with his whole life.

He inverted the conceptions and values not only of his own time but of all time. The deliverance he proclaimed was not a new *status* of salvation, a holy state in which one could rest secure. (It has often mistakenly been so understood!) It was rather release from futility into servanthood, a call to face the responsibility that inevitably accompanies freedom. The voluntary decision to make servanthood rather than domination one's way of life is the most vital choice one can make; but it must be steadily pursued in the endless series of day-to-day choices of which life is made up. It will not stay made once and for all.

So Jesus' steadfastness in the face of rejection and suffering and death is the measure of his faith-centered obedience. The Apostle Paul gave perfect expression to the inner meaning of the event as it is seen by those who come to God through him:

Let your bearing towards one another arise out of your life in Christ Jesus. For the divine nature was his from the first; yet he did not think to snatch at equality with God, but made himself nothing, assuming the nature of a slave. Bearing the human likeness, revealed in human shape, he humbled himself, and in obedience accepted even death—death on a cross. Therefore God raised him to the heights and bestowed on him the name above all names, that at the name of Jesus every knee should bow . . . and every tongue confess, "Jesus Christ is Lord," to the glory of God the Father. (Phil. 2:5-11, NEB)

"Jesus Christ is Lord." "God was in Christ reconciling the world to himself." These were the primary affirmations of the first generation of Christians—and of every generation including our own. Here, we believe, is the "point of authenticity" at which Christian disciples can meet men of other faiths. The elaboration of these affirmations across the centuries into creeds and doctrines is familiar to us, but not primary. For faith is not assent of the mind but committed allegiance of the will. If Jesus Christ is to speak *his* word to men of every faith and no faith, those who bear witness to him must follow the example of Paul, who proclaimed God's purpose to the Corinthians not with "brilliance of speech or intellect" but with a "secret determination to concentrate entirely on Jesus Christ himself and the fact of his death upon the cross," so that their faith would rest "not upon man's cleverness but upon the power of God." (1 Cor. 2:1-5)[7]

## THE CONTINUING PRESENCE

It is clear from the New Testament that the first generation of Christians were convinced that Jesus had not left them "without a comforter" but that he was among them as a spiritual presence, unseen but real. According to the apostolic tradition the day of Pentecost was the moment when "they were filled with the Holy Spirit," which came as "the rush of a mighty wind, and . . . filled all the house where they were sitting." (Acts 2:2-4) This event was crucial for the disciples, and thus for the church. It turned them from uncertainty and gloom to assurance and hope. It proved that God had vindicated Jesus and "made him both Lord and Christ." It made his continuing presence with them unmistakably certain. It set their task, that of witnessing to the mighty acts of God, and gave them both the power and the guidance to perform that task. In the light of this experience they perceived at a deeper level the significance of the life and death of Jesus. By the impulsion of the spirit the eleven disciples became apostles, "those who were sent," and those who received the word became the *ekklesia* (church), "the called assembly." But it was not a static community; they were quite literally what they called themselves, "the people of the Way." They were soon scattered by persecution, witnessing as they went.

As the word spread, the critical question in testing true discipleship became: "Have you received the Holy Spirit?" (See Acts 8:14-15) In hours of crisis Christians were conscious of being "filled with the Holy Spirit." They lived and acted in obedience to the Spirit. In the course of time the immediacy of this experience waned; it tended to be formal rather than vital. Some churches set great store by "gifts of the Spirit," of which ecstatic utterance was the most prized. These manifestations, carried to excess, became a source of confusion and division, which Paul sought to correct by a counteremphasis on the *fruits* of the Spirit: "love, joy, peace, patience, kindness, goodness, faithfulness, gentleness, self-control." (Gal. 5:22-23) But these were for him not mere attributes of a good and gracious personality but evidences of an overwhelming reality which he could only describe as being "in Christ," and as having the Spirit of Christ dwelling within. "But you are not in the flesh, you are in the Spirit, if the Spirit of God really dwells in you." (Rom. 8:9)

Probably few of Paul's contemporaries shared this experience of the living presence of Christ with the same intensity he felt. But it was certainly a reality to many of them, as it has been to many Christians in every generation, and as it is today. It is this experience which sustains and justifies the conviction that God is at work in the world through the lives of people who responded to his Spirit.

This conviction is itself grounded in faith; it can never be subjected to formal proof, even though some historians, like Kenneth Scott Latourette, may affirm that "at the very beginning of Christianity there . . . occurred a vast release of energy, unequalled in the history of the race."[8] It is clear that something happened to the men who associated with Jesus. Their assurance of his resurrection and of the continued living presence of his spirit with his disciples provided the initial dynamic of the Christian movement and has been transmitted to succeeding generations.

Theologians have tried to define the presence and work of the Spirit of God, but "the wind [the Spirit] blows where it wills." Human definitions cannot contain the living Spirit. Sacramentalists find him at the altar; mystics hear him in the silence of the waiting soul. Activists follow him into the strife of human encounter; monastics find him in the cloister. Those who suffer feel his healing touch, the weary find rest, the contrite pardon, the troubled peace. Many, in yielding their wills to him, find the whole course of their lives completely altered. All this together is formidable evidence that the presence of God with men is a reality. The cumulative experience of many generations of Christians cannot be explained away as self-delusion or mass hysteria. Possibly some new light may be thrown on the experience of spiritual awareness by depth psychology. Perhaps the mystical experience of men of other faiths may help Christians understand their own. But faith in God does not depend on such help. Despite all the skeptics and despite all inner doubts, Christians continue to declare: "I know in whom I have believed."

On the other hand, Christians cannot claim that the experience of God's presence is uniquely and exclusively theirs. The Bible makes no such claim; it teaches that the whole world is the realm of God's action and purpose, and that he is everywhere at work in it. The truth revealed in Christ is true everywhere, and not just within the church. The ultimacy of that revelation is not compromised by anything God has done or is doing among men who do not know the name of Christ. Only when Christians ascribe to the church a monopoly of God's grace do they mistakenly assert that "outside the church there is no salvation." The robust realism of secular thought challenges us to a more broadly sacramental understanding of reality. Thus it prepares the ground for a fresh encounter with men of other faiths.

Christ *is* the light of all men. Not all men know their light by that name, but such light as any of us has comes from him, however distorted by our dimness of vision. By his light the hidden mysteries of God will finally stand revealed. We must help one another to see more clearly.

For our knowledge is imperfect and our prophecy is imperfect; but when the perfect comes, the imperfect will pass away. . . . For now we see in a mirror dimly, but then face to face. Now I know in part; then I shall understand fully, even as I have been fully understood. (1 Cor. 13:9-10, 12)

# 6 *For the Healing of the Nations*

"AS THOU HAST SENT ME INTO THE WORLD, I HAVE sent them into the world." (John 17:18, NEB) These words are the marching orders of the Christian church. At the beginning of his ministry Jesus declared himself to be God's herald, bearing the good news of healing and release. At the end, in the shadow of the cross, he assigned this ministry to the disciples, and through them to all the succeeding generations of those "who through their words put their faith in [him]." (John 17:20, NEB)

In its essential nature, the church is the fellowship of those who accept this charge. It is—or should be—an intimate fellowship of mutual support and caring, for Jesus insistently urged the disciples to love one another. But it is an outward-facing fellowship, a body of envoys looking out and going out into the world. The church exists because Jesus Christ has come. It exists to proclaim the fact of his coming, to declare the great deeds of God in Christ not as something that *might* happen but as something that *has* happened and *is* happening. This is the great central conviction which alone has the toughness, resiliency, patience and endurance to undergird sustained missionary effort and make it effective.

As members of a witnessing fellowship spread abroad

through the whole world, Christians inevitably meet men of every faith and men of no faith. The question of how Christian faith relates to other faiths is inescapable. It affects not only the churches as corporate bodies engaged in declaring God's mighty acts in Christ but also every Christian in his attitudes toward other people, his judgments and decisions in daily life and his sense of vocation as a Christian. Every generation of Christians has wrestled with this question in terms of its own situation and its understanding of man and of the gospel.

Today, we wrestle with it in the context of a rapidly changing world. Christians, facing outward toward the world today, confront a bewildering scene. But Christians are not alone. Men of all faiths face a society in transition, and each one must ask himself what resources his faith can provide for worthy and effective living in this strange new world.

It is impossible to encompass all the factors that contribute to current social change in a brief statement. One recent analysis[1] mentions six conditions that are prevalent to some degree in most parts of the world:

1. *Revolution.* More than a billion people have undergone violent political upheaval since World War II. Nationalism, anticolonialism and social ferment keep half the nations of the world in turmoil.

2. *Population growth.* Population is rapidly outgrowing food supplies, health services, housing, schools, churches, water supplies—even land. Radical population control is imperative.

3. *Mobility.* Industry and the lure of city life are uprooting millions of people and transforming the culture even of those who stay behind. Old sanctions are weakened,

old loyalties displaced, old ties broken, old religious values destroyed. Every form of faith must discover afresh its relevance to new patterns and new settings for living.

4. *Need.* Social upheaval, war, famine and natural disasters create abysmal needs. A billion people are hungry. Multitudes are poor, sick, ignorant and devoid of hope. Development has been so uneven that while some nations are highly advanced, other peoples still have neither the resources nor the knowledge to improve their own conditions. And the gap steadily widens.

5. *Tension.* Recent history is a sorry tale of "superior" races dominating "inferior" peoples. As a result, hatred, injustice and discrimination abound. "The greatest human force in the world today is the dignity of the common man, his demand for recognition and status, his new hope and aspiration. We approach the time when all men must be free or none will be."

6. *Confusion.* Underlying and complicating all the other struggles is the struggle for men's minds.

Whether one thinks of the new ideological imperialism, more ruthless and devastating than colonial imperialism at its worst; or of sterile secularism without standards or hope; or the uncertainty that keeps men clutching at the broken reeds of nationalism or racism or of dead religions; or the dread of contemplating the awful destruction of power that we know how to create but lack the will to control; or just the plight of ordinary men who in the rush of change are in a sort of spiritual vacuum, with no relevant faith to live by: everywhere we face the struggle for men's minds and souls.

## A FAITH TO LIVE BY

This widespread confusion confronts us with the most challenging question of all: What is the relation between faith in the general sense of committed trust in God (or in the ultimate reality, however conceived) and a particular faith, a faith to live by? What guidance, what firm point of reference can religious faith provide to resolve the confusions, abate the tensions and meet the needs of this revolutionary world?

A particular faith obviously includes a particular understanding of God, man and the world. Christian faith affirms the mighty acts of God in Jesus Christ, not only as historical events but as grounds for knowing and trusting God. A faith *includes* a set of beliefs, but it is much more. It is a whole way of responding to reality, a frame of reference for living.

Such a frame of reference is important, for much of our present-day confusion stems from the necessity of living with uncertainty. This fact runs counter to the rational bias of Western culture. We like to act on the basis of knowledge. We say: "Get the facts, verify the evidence, understand the whole situation, then you will know what to do." We tend to exalt knowledge unduly, forgetting that it can be perverted to selfish and evil ends. Motives are at least as important as facts in reaching sound judgments. And the truth is that we can never wait for all the data to come in before we act. At every moment of our lives we have to make irrevocable decisions on the basis of the best information and judgment we can bring to bear at that time.

A faith to live by is a view of life and reality that provides an adequate frame of reference for the process of decision making, which lies at the very root of personality. A person is not always conscious of either the process or the frame of reference, but both are always present, underlying judgment and action. To be really adequate a person's faith must provide a way of looking at the world that unifies experience into a meaningful whole. It must subject personal hopes and hungers to the discipline of loyal collaboration with others in pursuit of common purposes. It must channel the drive of what has been called "the will to dominate" into the service of "the will to self-realization through self-giving."

A person can hold his Christian beliefs as abstract formulas—hold them at arm's length, so to speak—and remain without a faith to live by. But a true commitment of the whole being to God in Christ can indeed provide an inner force and focus. To those who have been confused, broken, defeated and torn with tensions, such a faith brings new wholeness. In the most literal sense an individual is healed by faith. This, at the personal level, is the healing work of Christ. He began it during his earthly ministry and through his church he graciously continues it throughout history. For *healing* is the root meaning of the Greek word commonly translated "salvation."

## THE HEALING MINISTRY OF THE CONGREGATION

The primary task of the church, now and always, is to share ever more widely this experience of healing and renewal through committed faith in God. Until recently, the healing (or "saving") ministry of the congregation in its community would have been understood in one or both of two senses. On the one hand, it would have meant winning people to personal commitment to Christ and drawing them into the fellowship of the congregation. On the other hand, it would have meant engaging in welfare and service activities for the public good along scores of well-known lines. Both these ministries, personal and social, are valid and necessary.

But now a third dimension is being rediscovered, which is, quite literally, the congregational ministry of healing, or "making whole." The wholeness with which we are concerned includes physical and mental healing, as far as they are attainable. It includes liberation from the dominion of fear into confident acceptance of suffering and death as the transition to larger life. It includes recovery of wholesome relations with other people and a sense of direction and purpose in life. The congregation, being the local fellowship of God's people, is the cell, the core group, primarily responsible for the health (in this broad sense) of its own members and for a healing ministry in the community. We have learned that *the congregation itself has a ministry of healing both through the mutual concern of its members for one another's well being and through their shared concern for the corporate life of the community.*

This larger understanding of the congregational ministry of healing was underscored at a recent consultation held at Tübingen, Germany, in 1964. Starting as a consultation with specialized medical and psychiatric personnel and institutions, the group found itself coming suddenly to a new insight:

Health, in the Christian understanding . . . is a kind of life which has overcome death and the anxiety which is the shadow of death. Whether in the desperate squalor of overpopulated and underdeveloped areas, or in the spiritual wasteland of affluent societies, it is a sign of God's victory and a summons to his service. . . .

If healing is understood [in this inclusive sense] the entire congregation has a part to play in it. By its prayer, by the love with which it surrounds each person, by the practical acts, which express its concern for every man, and by the opportunities which it offers for participation in Christ's mission, the congregation is the primary agent of healing. At the heart of this healing activity lies the ministry of the Word, sacraments and prayer. The specialized work of [trained medical personnel] . . . have their proper place and will be [fully] fruitful in the context of this whole congregational life.[2]

The full significance of this insight is only beginning to appear. As our understanding of "healing" in strictly scientific, medical, almost mechanistic terms gives way to this more personal understanding of healing as the "making whole" of the entire person, it ought to be possible to reunite the medical and spiritual aspects of healing. Certain churches in Africa boldly experimenting with healing ministries, expressed in terms consistent both with African conceptions of health and disease and with the Christian faith. For people only now emerging from animism, such a bridge is immensely important. Perhaps it may be possible to provide comparable ministries of transition and adjustment in many other situations of change and mobility throughout the world.

Even more important, this new insight should do much to give renewed substance to the corporate life of the churches.

## CHRISTIAN DIALOGUE WITH MEN OF OTHER FAITHS

Both the Christian as a person who has a faith to live by and the church as a healed and healing fellowship are obligated to share their experience with others. This obligation is not an optional extra step of obedience to a particular command of Jesus Christ; it is intrinsic to the nature of faith and truth. It is part of the experience of committed trust. But at this point many Christians have doubts and hesitations.

In any other realm than religion people feel free to commend to others the experiences they value. "Be sure to read X, it is a wonderful book!" "Be sure to visit Z, we had a fine vacation there." "Go to doctor A, he helped me immensely." Furthermore, we are usually ready to back up our opinions with reasons. We are ready to discuss, to analyze, to argue and debate the merits or faults of the point at issue. This is the normal, wholesome process of sharing experience, which results in consensus and community consciousness.

A refinement of the same process is used in reaching scientific consensus. New findings often seem to call in question established "truth." But they are discussed and retested, theories are proposed to reconcile the new and the old, and gradually a new synthesis emerges in which all the known facts are seen as a consistent whole.

For various reasons we hesitate to discuss issues of faith and religion with the same degree of freedom. It is true that faith is an intensely personal matter. A person does not willingly open the private world of his intimate selfhood to public inspection; yet his intimate self is the one that needs healing. The private world can be the prison and the private hell of a tormented soul, or a desert wasteland in which a lost, disoriented person wanders aimlessly. In such cases the need for healing is obvious, and anyone who is able to breach the wall of isolation with compassionate concern and healing power has an obvious responsibility to do so.

Generally the need is less acute, but no less real. The reticence, in our culture, to talk about matters of faith seems to be a kind of prudery not unlike the conspiracy of silence in matters of sex that was in vogue a generation or two ago. Like the latter, it is unwholesome, depriving people not only of information but of an opportunity to grow into healthy maturity by sharing the wonder and unfolding beauty of a profound human experience. In both cases it is not silence but objectivity that is needed—the objectivity of knowledge held in common with others as the basis of decisions and commitments that each person must make for himself.

Objective study of religion and open discussion of faith as a way of understanding life are good and necessary. Coercion, on the other hand, especially at the deep level of personal commitment, is wrong. "Conversion" has a bad name mainly because this distinction has been ignored. Churches seek members. They welcome newcomers, as they should. They proclaim the gospel, as they should. But *when the proclamation of the gospel becomes primarily a device for adding members to the church, the whole meaning of the gospel is lost.* Self-concern for the church as an institution supplants healing concern for persons in need of a faith to live by.

The search for *truth* and *faith* and *fellowship* is a valid function of the church and its members; but the three objectives of that search are separate and distinct, and should not be confused with one another. For people who do not find in a particular religious community the grounds for a mature and satisfying faith to live by, the quest for "faith" is the quest for truth, in the sense of a meaningful way of looking at life, rather than for a specifically "religious" belief. Membership in a religious body may or may not seem relevant for such people; certainly, constraint to join or to remain a member of any church can frequently be harmful.

Finding truth is aided by open study and discussion. Genuine confrontation between people of different points of view is wholesome and should be encouraged. But such discussion must be frank and fearless. It dare not rule out some subjects on the ground that "authority has spoken and closed the issue," or that "different presuppositions make agreement impossible." Such defensiveness is likely to be interpreted as an admission that the views in question have no sure basis at all. Robust faith is built upon convictions, based in knowledge and experience, that will stand the scrutiny of debate.

Deep sensitivities are involved, however, and direct inter-faith discussions may not always be possible. In particular, discussions *in the context of a church* may not be free from an element of coercion. Even the fact of living in a certain society, with its particular social mores and assumptions, is a coercive influence tending to favor the prevailing majority religious viewpoint. For instance, Jewish sensitivities in the United States reflect the defensiveness of a minority fearful of losing its own identity. There are two ways to handle the problem. Orthodox Jews often prefer to restrict interfaith relations to social and moral issues, excluding theological discussion on the ground that there can be no mutual understanding about such topics, because Jew and Christian use different categories, frames of reference, and standards of evaluation. Leaders of Conservative and Reform Judaism take the opposite view, and engage in dialogue in the hope of better understanding among the religious communities.

Secular pressures are beginning to overcome such hesitations. Clamant human need makes practical interfaith cooperation necessary, and personal fellowship breaks down barriers. Muslims have generally been extremely reluctant to engage in religious dialogue with Christians in situations where any possibility of a desire to convert could be suspected. Centuries of mutual antagonism have reinforced this attitude. But Westerners of Christian background, working on problems of national development in a remote, totally Muslim community in Asia, may find themselves searching the *Qur'an,* along with the local religious leaders, for texts that will lend support to the social changes they want to introduce. Such instances signify the necessity of revitalizing the religions—if that is possible—in order to find within them a relevant faith for today. This effort may be only partially successful, but the very fact that it is beginning to be made marks a new stage in interfaith relations.

A movement of greater scope is the provision under Christian auspices of centers for the study of religion and society. Such study centers now exist in Asia at Bangalore and Jabalpur, India; Jaffna, Ceylon; Hong Kong; Kyoto, Japan; and Manila, the Philippines. There is one in the Near East, one at Algiers, one at Ibadan, Nigeria, and one at Kitwe, Zambia. And in Latin America there is one at Montevideo, Uruguay. There are also the Ecumenical Institute at Bossey, Switzerland, and a number of other centers in the Western world. These study centers engage Christian and non-Christian scholars and students in the exploration together of a wide range of issues at the frontiers where faith and religion confront the social, cultural and political realities of our time. Each center develops its own program along lines congenial to the national culture. Most of them publish periodical reviews or bulletins as well as occasional books and pamphlets.

These centers provide a type of Christian affirmation in relation to each of the major religions which can only be made from within the culture: restatements of Christian faith and truth in language and thought forms congenial to the people of that land and culture. Beyond that, they aim to focus on the relation of faith to life—to set social needs in a cogent religious frame of reference. Christian faith *is* relevant, as we have seen. How far the prevailing religion of the area is congenial to a vital faith to live by is always the dominant question, as it is for everyone, East or West, North or South. Paul D. Clasper, writing in Burma, makes the point clear:

In Burma we live amidst a variety of the most time-honoured religions of mankind. There are many roads which one can follow. But all these different roads have one thing in common. They are marked by one sign: "Save Yourself By Yourself." *But is there any other way?* . . . Paul saw clearly . . . the contrast between *religions,* as man's own unaided effort to achieve the good life, and the *good news* of an alternative way—God's love-gift of eternal life through Jesus Christ . . . that through the surrender of oneself, or the opening of life to this love of God, one entered the new life in Christ. . . .[3]

Christians are prone to forget this distinction. Like people of other faiths, they tend to think of religion as a way of manipulating the powers of the spiritual realm for their own ends. Bishop Stephen F. Bayne, Jr. has put the matter succinctly:

It is the essence of "religion" to choose God, a good man-ageable God who will "stay on the reservation." . . . Indeed a great deal of American religion . . . is occupied with keeping God in business. [Don't we think that] "if we don't stick with

God he is not going to have any friends in this place"? He has
been kicked out of Russia and China. . . . Little by little his
sphere is being contracted and it is the duty of American Christians to patronize him. . . . We have chosen God and this is
precisely what "religion" means. A patronizing of God, a
placating of God, a using of God, a domesticating of God.
Those who rebel in favor of a religionless Christianity are rightly
rebelling against this. Man has always rebelled against this as
our Lord himself rebelled against it. It may be doubted whether
Christianity is a religion at all. It develops religious people—
some good, some bad—but the heart of Christianity is not a
religion. The heart of Christianity is a Person who chooses us
to be his friends.[4]

Hence the dialogue is not primarily between people of
different *religions.* The dialogue, *even within the churches,*
is between those who want to use religion for their own
ends and those who are ready to let God use them for his
ends—between religious worldlings and the committed people of God.

What will be the outcome of these efforts to express the
good news of Jesus Christ more cogently? We do not yet
know. Interfaith dialogue should improve understanding
and reduce prejudice, making the way easier for those
whose convictions impel them to an open profession of faith
in God through Jesus Christ. It should restore the possibility of personal faith to the people—literally millions of
people, be they Muslims or Hindus or animists or Buddhists,
or Christians—whose encounter with secularism and science
has swept them off their feet. For the old wineskins of
traditional religion cannot contain the heady ferment of new
knowledge and new hope. But we cannot rule out the
further possibility that ancient faiths may be renewed from
within by the word of life which Christ brought into the
world. St. Paul dared to assert that *"all things* are put in

subjection under him." (1 Cor. 15:27) Does this not include the ancient faiths and religious traditions of men?
Already his influence is incalculable. Who would dare set
a limit to what it may become?

It has nearly always been assumed that faith in Christ
entails church membership as a matter of course. This
assumption may not be fully justified. Some societies are
rigidly structured into separate communities; for example,
the castes in India and the millets in the Middle East.
Each community is a self-contained social, economic and
cultural unit; it is a "nation" within the nation. To be cast
out of the community deprives one of citizenship, livelihood,
family relationships and cultural ties. While a few rare
souls have made this extreme sacrifice for Christ, one may
ask whether their exclusion does in fact promote either the
glory of God or the progress of the gospel. Is it not more
truly the calling of a committed disciple of Christ to remain
within his community, living out his faith as he can and
sharing it with others in the hope that the whole community
will find itself impelled to acknowledge a change of allegiance? It is certain that a growing number of self-styled
Christians remain within the predominantly Buddhist,
Jainist, Hindu and other religious groups of Asia, and outside the churches. If this is the form of obedience to which
God calls certain people, should there not be some way of
recognizing and confirming them in it?

Presumably the answer should be "Yes," though how
this can be done has not been adequately worked out. The
challenge to the individual is clear enough. He must become a member of the healing fellowship. But this puts
the onus entirely on the lonely disciple. And the healing
community needs to face its own challenge. How can it

extend the bounds of its fellowship to embrace and sustain those whose faith commitment is to Christ, but whose cultural ties bind them to a predominantly non-Christian society? Only as a completely open group, standing over against all the other closed groups, can it become a pervasive force reaching into every group and transforming them from within. Only so can the church *be* the healing community. It must be ready to sacrifice its selfhood, its visible identity as a corporate body, by an act of glad surrender to the Spirit who moves out beyond the frontiers of human planning and the boundaries of human compartmentalization.

This is the reason Bishop Hassan Dehgani-Tafti of Iran writes:

To me there is no contradiction in such a term as "Muslim-Christian," "Hebrew-Christian" or "Zoroastrian-Christian." A Zoroastrian cannot help being a Zoroastrian, but he can baptize his Zoroastrianness into Christ. He must not be made to feel ashamed of what he really is, he need not be pushed to forget all his customs and ways of life, he must not be encouraged to change his name. . . . The splendour and the glory of Christianity is that it could bring into one free fellowship all manners of people. God is against uniformity. He wants unity of spirit in diversity of souls. Any Church must be part and parcel of the nation in which she is living and not a closed ghetto.[5]

Some radically secular segments of Western society— some industrial communities, inner cities, migrant labor camps, certain universities—are as resistant to evangelization as any pagan culture. At best there is indifference, at worst open hostility to the church. Here too a style of life that might be called "secular Christianity" or "anonymous discipleship" seems to be a form of Christian obedience to which some are called—the French worker priests are a case in point. More courageous pioneering is certainly called for. Answers have yet to be found.

There seems to be a contradiction between the idea of "anonymous discipleship," or of Christians who remain within the culture-group of their own people, on the one hand, and the idea of the church universal as the one people of God united in faith and fellowship, on the other. This is perhaps more apparent than real. Bishop Dehgani-Tafti points toward the answer in suggesting that unity of spirit is consistent with diversity of souls, and that God does not want uniformity. Most of our existing denominations originated as adaptations of the common Christian heritage to the particular needs or viewpoints of a specific nation or culture group. In many instances the reason for their separateness no longer exists; the actual unity of the people of God transcends these apparent cleavages. But there is need today for "cells of faith and witness" whose members seek to maintain an active "Christian presence" within every segment of society. The church must learn to understand and sustain such people in their special callings, even when their style of life is far from orthodox.

All this indicates something of the range of interfaith dialogue now taking place and the issues involved. Much more is needed; for every Christian lives at the frontier between faith and unfaith. (To be honest, the frontier is within us, because faith involves a commitment *beyond what we know to him in whom we trust.*) We are all in daily contact with people with whom our conversation should be, in some sense, Christian dialogue.

The conversation about the Christian faith is often most meaningfully conducted in the simple perspective of men in their secular lives. In the last analysis, the Christian encounter is an encounter with men as men, both in their religious life and in their non-religious life, both in their belief and in their unbelief, both in what they hold to be sacred and in what they hold to be secular.[6]

The whole church, therefore, all its members and not just its clergy, is charged with declaring the gospel of Christ to a world which is basically pagan and at the same time the arena of God's concern. How can it be done?

## THE CORPORATE WITNESS OF THE CHURCH

The church is present in the world in a variety of ways. It is most visibly present in the form of tens of thousands of worshiping congregations throughout the world. Generally the congregation has its house of worship—the church building—with suitable annexes for educational and social activities. To most people in America, no doubt, the word "church" means first of all a building and what goes on inside it. Secondly, it means the body of people who frequent the place; and "church life" means the things they do there together. Thirdly, "church" means the denominational grouping which links together congregations of the same historic strain of Christian tradition. The denominational body includes boards and agencies for the common needs and interests of the congregations. It provides organs—synods, conferences, assemblies, conventions and the like—through which the common mind of the whole fellowship can be formed, expressed and acted upon. The church, in this sense, has a voice in the public life of the nation, especially in open democratic societies. At various levels from the local congregation to the denomination, churches relate to one another across denominational lines in councils of churches. These enable the churches to engage in more effective consultation, study, planning and action together. Councils help the churches reach consensus on major issues and facilitate united action locally, nationally and internationally. There is no doubt that the emergence of a World Council of Churches embracing some two hundred Protestant and Orthodox churches was one of the factors that led to the convening of the Second Vatican Council. That Council, in turn, set in motion a radical reorientation of the Roman Catholic Church, from a rather introverted, backward-looking communion to an outward-facing, courageous church eager to bring Christian faith to bear on all the moral and social issues of the day. New possibilities thus exist for concerted Christian study, reflection and consensus on a scale never before possible.

These large-scale structures give the churches a public voice and a public image. It is of primary importance that they should express *public* concern—direct human concern for people in every situation—rather than promote the private interests of the churches themselves. The task of the churches is to witness *for God* (not for themselves) in respect to every human need, every moral and social issue. The churches must be *participants* in the struggles of mankind. Pronouncements from the sidelines have a palpable falsity that nullifies their significance. The witness of words must be confirmed by the witness of *credible acts*—acts undertaken not for the sake of demonstration but under the impulsion of self-sacrificing love.

The historic involvement of the churches in schools and education, hospitals and medical service, social work and welfare activities has been an impressive witness of Christian concern in action. Now that governments are increasingly, and properly, assuming major responsibility for such services, the share borne by private agencies has been reduced, though there is still much more to be done than all agencies together, public and private, can accomplish. Any church staff or any resources released at one point are immediately needed somewhere else. Furthermore, there is always need for experimental, pioneering work on the frontiers of knowledge and service. As the churches once pioneered in providing schools and hospitals, they have more recently taken bold initiatives in service to refugees and migrants, disaster relief, service to the blind, the crippled, the illiterate and other handicapped persons, famine relief, rural reconstruction, urban renewal, emergency aid to victims of war, and many other areas. Church agencies are always ready to respond immediately to the cry of need. They are mobilized for emergency action, either by themselves or with others. For operations over a longer term and on a large scale the collaboration of governments or public corporations is essential, both to provide sufficient resources and to develop such programs into long-term public services. Churches cannot and should not do everything that needs to be done for the common good. Their readiness to respond to new, emerging needs, to pioneer and point the way in meeting them, and to give place to others in due course is an outstanding contribution to "the healing of the nations." It is witness in action to the mind and spirit of Jesus Christ.

One particular phase of Christian concern and witness must be mentioned: the field of international relations and the quest for peace. The people of God are a worldwide fellowship whose primary loyalty to the Prince of Peace transcends national divisions. Christians are conscious that any international conflict divides the household of faith, as it does the family of man, setting brother against brother. War is inherently evil. Some churches espouse pacifism as a matter of principle. Few Christians anywhere would regard the ancient doctrine of the "just war" as applicable today. The causes of conflict are too complex to be resolved on moralistic grounds; right is never all on one side. Hence the weight of Christian judgment, taking the world as a whole, is strongly on the side of conciliation in any threatened conflict.

These facts do not of themselves give the churches or their members competence in international relations. They do lead the churches to concern themselves with issues that threaten peace or deny freedom to any people. This concern expresses itself in many ways: among them friendly visits, interpretation of opposing viewpoints, study commissions, deputations, public pronouncements and representations to governments. The Commission of the Churches on International Affairs of the World Council of Churches and related national commissions, together with corresponding Roman Catholic agencies, are beginning to give such action a new coherence and a weight of emphasis for conciliation and peace.

## WITNESS BY PERSONAL INVOLVEMENT

It is not always the church as a visible body—a corporate entity—that is best able to express its faith in action. More often than not it is the Christian as citizen, through his personal involvement in secular affairs and in the corporate structures of secular society. This arena of Christian witness and action is by far the most important. It is also the least understood, the least explored, the least defined. For our habits of thought about the life of the church have turned our minds inward rather than outward.

Let us look again at the congregation, the people of God gathered together for worship. We are part of this congregation. What are we doing here? By a curious misuse of language which is almost as old as the church, our act of corporate worship is called "divine service." But is this where God needs to be served? What did Jesus say? "As Thou hast sent me into the world, so have I sent them into the world." The congregation comes together to receive strength and guidance—rations and marching orders—from its Lord. It *goes out* of the sanctuary to serve God *in the world.*

The church's mission begins, not with the church, but with God, who has called us and chosen us. He is out ahead of us, calling us to find our way with him. The question is not how the laity, or the laity and clergy together, can best help the church serve the world. The question is: What is God doing in the world, and how can we be at his side? In the words of Bishop Bayne, "The job of the Christian is to be Christ in our time and place, within the limits of our finitude, within the limits of our sin, but still to be Christ, the friend, and so to make him known and loved and believed in by those who do not know him."[7]

It is manifestly impossible to describe the specific way in which any one of us carries out this ministry, because in each case it is our response to people in a particular situation. It is not just "being good." It is not what we are in any abstract sense, but what we do in specific circumstances. It is in positions that we take and things that we do. It is necessary, for example, for Christians in our time to be accused of being "nigger lovers." Because ministry means taking positions and doing things, it brings evil report and good report. We cannot escape the complex of ambiguity.

The "complex of ambiguity" is another way of expressing the burden of making decisions responsibly, with courageous regard for others, when the issues are not sharply drawn. "Who is my neighbor?" asked the lawyer. And Jesus replied with a story that stretched the term to its widest possible meaning. Not the man in the house next door—as we usually think of a neighbor. Not in the neighborhood at all, but on the open road. Not an acquaintance but a stranger. Not a fellow countryman but a foreigner. The neighbor was the man who saw a fellowman in need and helped him. He went beyond the call of conventional obligation, he turned aside from his own interests. He spent and gave and enlisted the services of others. This is the prototype of the ministry of the laity, regardless of the form it takes with any of us, for the form is unpredictable.

An immense amount of such ministry takes place constantly, humbly, quietly, without fanfare or commotion. And yet there is certainly room for much more. The strange thing is that this direct, spontaneous, active witness of friendship is often regarded as a marginal extra to the business of being a Christian, when in fact it is the very substance of it.

To illustrate: The Willingen meeting of the International Missionary Council in 1952 discussed the ever-increasing number of Christians living and working outside their own countries. The suggestion was made that some of them might reinforce the missionary outreach of the churches by serving as "lay missionaries," while carrying out their business or professional assignments. This idea proved remarkably unworkable, for two reasons. First, it assumed that a line could be drawn between Christians who are called to bear witness to their faith and those who are not. To formalize the appointment of some implied the release of the others from their calling to "be doers of the Word and not hearers only." Second, it assumed that the churches could point out work to be done and assign tasks. But real witness takes place in the context not of the church but of the world.

A recent inquiry into the ways Christian laymen overseas have been finding to manifest their faith in the context of their life in the world brought revealing results. Obviously the environment itself is a test. People sent overseas have to adjust to a foreign cultural and religious climate, sometimes to difficult living conditions, to unfamiliar and perplexing social and business relationships. But they are chosen to go overseas with these factors in mind and they are expected to be able to cope with any situation that should arise.

Laymen express their Christian commitment through "worldly" initiative. One such person is an engineer who is working to develop electrical cooperatives in a Latin American country. He has such a passion to serve the people in the villages that he has become a one-man expediter of the whole operation. One day he may be working with his hands beside the local laborers; the next, he may be tracking down missing equipment or encouraging local officials who hesitate to take action. There are, too, women joining forces to find food, clothes, medicines, bottles and other supplies for the desperately poor, and establishing a health clinic for children. In one country there is a group of thirty who have banded themselves together as "the fellowship of the concerned," with small funds but tremendous influence to reinforce the work of missionaries among poor and backward people. Prayer groups have been formed, in which local and foreign executives and professional people meet together and share their common Christian social concern. Other examples include a businessman who applies a share of his profits to help maladjusted individuals; persons who initiate community groups to promote social action in mass housing developments; a surgeon who is regarded as a "saint in a white jacket"—and many others.

But there are also many who take a different approach to life in a foreign country, who cherish only their job, their status and their salary. Some avoid involvement, not wanting to put roots down anywhere. As a result, writes one minister, "they will probably go through life rootless as far as the church or any other community interest is concerned. Parties, yes; travel to the mountains and beaches, yes; fishing, yes; but church or community service, no."

The comment of one correspondent was extremely revealing:

There are several in our community who bear a wholesome Christian witness but who don't fit the conventional church type. They hold cocktail parties, and yet are most effective in the community. They are honest, well-liked and talented. I think of them as the worldly pious.

I have the feeling that we too often look for stereotypes; we think of Christian witness largely in terms of Bible reading, prayer, assisting the congregations. It is often the worldly pious who have the best relationship with others. But they don't use the conventional language of the church, and some of them don't come very often. But those persons—unconsciously Christian or living off inherited spiritual capital—are our allies.[8]

True Christian witness in action is never stereotyped. It breaks out in spontaneous response to each new situation. And some who do not seem responsive may stand ready, waiting only for the moment when their particular call to action comes. Nor should we overstress the role of Western Christians abroad. There is mutual giving and taking everywhere. One recalls an African graduate student in an American university who challenged the secular bias of his teachers by showing how Christian faith was changing the culture and viewpoint of his own people. One hears of a Hindu youth in Europe who feels that he must remain a Hindu, but who voluntarily leads a Christian youth program because "all his altruism comes from reading the Christian Scriptures and from fellowship with Christians." Or one thinks of the late Mohandas Gandhi, who learned nonviolence in South Africa from the teachings of Jesus and applied it to the liberation of India. His example in turn has inspired both American and African Negro leaders in their own struggles for freedom, and the end is not yet.

Nor must we forget the simple and humble people throughout the world who in their own quiet ways work the works of God, do good, heal the brokenhearted and testify by their lives to the faith that is in them. To name but a single one, there is in Tokyo a Christian shoemaker who is also a poet. In his shoe repair stand in the corridor of a girls' school there are always scraps of paper bearing his poems—poems about familiar things like the odor of work clothing to a small boy's nostrils, the prattling of a baby to its mother, a whistle on a factory roof. As his work gained notice he persuaded others to write, especially those who faced with near despair, as he once did, the prospect of a lifetime of ordinary labor. His congregation has helped found a publication, *Clouds and Barley,* which now has 135 regular contributors—workingmen, housewives and students —who meet twice a month for mutual criticism under his guidance. Here is a translation of one of his poems:

> All I want
> Is a heart well-water clear
> With innocence,
> Fit to make an honest poem.
>
> All I want
> Is courage to expose myself
> Innocently, on happy
>   and unhappy occasions
> To my God.
>
> All I want
> Is a heart and will to believe
> Innocently.[9]

Thus in many ways, great and small, the testimony of the spoken word is confirmed by acts of witness. Whatever the partial faith and partial insight with which we approach God, whatever the religious tradition out of which we come, Jesus Christ fulfills and transcends it. He, beyond any other, speaks to the true condition of man. He alone is the Liberator, the Healer, the Source of life and truth. His Spirit, continuing among men, nerves the soul to face reality unafraid and to spend itself utterly in the service of others. The fulfillment of God's purpose is yet to be, but already we can see from afar with the eyes of hope the vision of the City of God.

. . . the glory of God is its light, and its lamp is the Lamb. By its light shall the nations walk; and the kings of the earth shall bring their glory into it. . . . Then [I beheld] the river of the water of life, bright as crystal, flowing from the throne of God and of the Lamb . . . [and] the tree of life with its twelve kinds of fruit, yielding its fruit each month; and the leaves of the tree were for the healing of the nations. (Rev. 21:23—22:2)

## EPILOGUE: ON THE ACTION OF GOD IN HISTORY

Does our study lead to any clear conclusions as to how God acts in the history of our time? I believe it does, and I would make the following affirmations:

1. We cannot know the whole purpose of God, but one thing at least is clear: he proposes to raise up for himself a human race able to bear the burden of increasing freedom and use that freedom responsibly for the common good. Jesus Christ is the prototype of that new humanity.

2. Every new truth, every valid insight, every increment of power over nature is a gift of God within the context of this liberating purpose. Every such gift entails responsibility for its use. Misused it becomes destructive; rightly used it enhances both man's freedom and his power to serve the common good. All men are involved together in receiving God's gifts and learning to use them for the common good of all.

3. Christians are those who have accepted the call to live as citizens of the new order of humanity within the old. They are "first fruits" of that which is to come. In them the future begins to be present. Their special function is to pioneer in the transformation of society—of human character and relations—which alone can make man's increasing domination of the material world beneficial to mankind.

4. To serve this end Christians must have a special responsiveness to the promptings of the Holy Spirit, "an open-

ness on the Godward side," which enables God to use them as instruments of his purpose. In the words of Bonhoeffer, such responsiveness is "costly grace."

Costly grace is the treasure hidden in the field; for the sake of it a man will gladly go and sell all that he has. It is the pearl of great price to buy which the merchant will sell all his goods. It is the kingly rule of Christ, for whose sake a man will pluck out the eye which causes him to stumble, it is the call of Jesus Christ at which the disciple leaves his nets and follows him. . . .

Such grace is *costly* because it calls us to follow, and it is *grace* because it calls us to follow *Jesus Christ*. It is costly because it costs a man his life, and it is grace because it gives a man the only true life. Costly grace is the Incarnation of God.[10]

# FOOTNOTES

CHAPTER 1

¹Dietrich Bonhoeffer, *Prisoner for God: Letters and Papers from Prison.* New York: Macmillan, and London: SCM Press, 1961, pp. 122-123.

²*Ibid.*, pp. 15-16.

³Those who wish to pursue this analysis further will find an excellent discussion of it in *The Meaning and End of Religion,* by Wilfred Cantwell Smith. New York: Macmillan, 1962.

⁴Bonhoeffer, *op. cit.*, p. 179.

⁵*Rig-Veda,* Book X, 129.

⁶Dag Hammarskjöld, *Markings.* Translated from the Swedish by Leif Sjöberg and W. H. Auden. New York: Alfred A. Knopf, 1964, p. 205.

⁷Quoted in Gerald Anderson, *The Theology of the Christian Mission.* New York: McGraw Hill, 1961, p. 146.

⁸Nels Ferré, *The Finality of Faith.* New York: Harper & Row, 1963, p. 9.

⁹*The Meaning of History,* Copyright 1964 by Erich Kahler. Reprinted by permission of George Braziller, Inc.

¹⁰Padipedi Chenchiah, "Christianity and Non-Christian Faiths," in *Relations Among Religions Today,* Moses Jung (ed.). Leiden; E. J. Brill, 1963, p. 64.

¹¹Rudolph Bultmann, *Jesus and the Word.* New York: Scribner's, 1958, p. 50.

¹²New York: Macmillan, and London: Epworth Press, 1953, pp. 40-41.

CHAPTER 2

¹deBary, Chann and Watson (eds.), *Oriental Civilizations: Sources of Chinese Tradition*. New York: Columbia University Press, 1960, p. 15.

²Eugene A. Nida and William A. Smalley, *Introducing Animism*. New York: Friendship Press, 1959, p. 29.

³Ernst Cassirer, *An Essay on Man*. New Haven: Yale University Press, 1944, p. 225.

⁴In *The Religion of the Hindus*, edited by Kenneth W. Morgan. Copyright 1953, The Ronald Press Company, New York.

⁵Taittiriya Aranyaka, X. 48. Quoted in *Ibid.*, pp. 291-292.

⁶*Ibid.*, p. 153.

⁷*Ibid.*

⁸deBary, et al., *op. cit.*, p. 307.

⁹*CMS Newsletter*, July 1965, No. 284, p. 1.

¹⁰P. D. Devanandan, *The Gospel and Renascent Hinduism* (IMC Research Pamphlet No. 8). London: SCM Press, 1959, pp. 55-57.

CHAPTER 3

¹From *A Faith for the Nations* by Charles W. Forman. Copyright 1957, W. L. Jenkins. The Westminster Press. Used by permission.

²*Op. cit.*, pp. 42-44.

³Eugene L. Smith, "Ecumenical Perspective on Judaism," in *Ecumenical Review*, Vol. XVII, No. 4, p. 350.

⁴Dag Hammarskjöld, *op. cit.*, pp. 68-69.

⁵Kenneth Cragg, *The Call of the Minaret*. New York: Oxford University Press, 1956, pp. 93, 94.

[6]*Ibid.,* pp. 46-48, passim.

[7]*Ibid.,* pp. 36, 37.

[8]Sura 19, quoted in Najib Ullah, *Islamic Literature.* New York: Washington Square Press, 1963, pp. 22-23.

[9]Eugene L. Smith, *op. cit.,* p. 355.

[10]Daud Rahbar, "Muslims and the Finality of Jesus Christ," in *Ecumenical Review,* Vol XVII, No. 4, p. 360.

[11]*Ibid.,* pp. 362-363.

[12]Eugene L. Smith, *op. cit.,* pp. 358-359.

CHAPTER 4

[1]deBary, et al., *op. cit.,* p. 612.

[2]*Ibid.,* p. 590.

[3]John J. Considine, M. M., *The Church in the New Latin America.* Notre Dame, Indiana: Fides Publishers, 1964, p. 20.

[4]David M. Stowe, "The Shape of Our Calling to Mission," address at Nashville Assembly, Division of Overseas Ministries, NCC, October 1965.

[5]*Our Mission Today.* New York: World Outlook, 1963, pp. 49-50.

[6]J. B. Phillips, *The New Testament in Modern English.* New York: Macmillan, 1958.

[7]"Will Man Direct His Own Evolution?" *Reader's Digest,* January 1966, p. 37.

CHAPTER 5

[1]*Challenge and Response.* New York: Morehouse-Barlow, 1959, pp. 16-17.

[2]*Ibid.,* p. 8.

[3]*Ibid.,* p. 17.

[4]Joachim Jeremias, *The Problem of the Historical Jesus.* Philadelphia: Fortress Press, 1964, pp. 20-21.

[5]Reinhold Niebuhr, *The Children of Light and the Children of Darkness.* New York: Scribner's, 1944, pp. 20-23.

[6]Rudolph Bultmann, *op. cit.,* pp. 83-84.

[7]J. B. Phillips, *The New Testament in Modern English.*

[8]Kenneth Scott Latourette, *A History of the Expansion of Christianity.* New York: Harper & Row, 1937, Vol. I, pp. 167-168.


CHAPTER 6

[1]United Presbyterian Church in the U.S.A., *Plan for Planning prepared by the Joint Planning Staff of the Committee on Long Range Planning,* 1966 (adapted and summarized). Both the quotations in the first section of this chapter are from the preliminary draft of this document.

[2]*The Healing Church.* Geneva: World Council of Churches, 1965, pp. 35-36.

[3]*New Life in Christ.* London: Lutterworth (World Christian Books) and New York: Association Press, 1961, pp. 8, 9.

[4]In *The Layman's Share,* Report of the North American Conference on the Ministry of the Laity in the World, January 1966, p. 12.

⁵Hassan Dehgani-Tafti, *The Art of Being a Christian Minority in Iran.* Address at the Consultation on Religious Liberty in Muslim Countries, July 1965.

⁶*Christian Encounter with Men of Other Beliefs.* East Asia Christian Conference, Bangkok Assembly Statement, 1964, p. 3.

⁷Stephen F. Bayne, *op. cit.,* pp. 12-13.

⁸From a personal letter.

⁹Yoshihiko Ujino. Copyright 1966 by *Presbyterian Life.* Used by permission.

¹⁰Dietrich Bonhoeffer, *The Cost of Discipleship.* New York: Macmillan, and London: SCM Press, 1959, pp. 36-37.

# SUPPLEMENTARY READING

SPECIFIC RELIGIONS

Appleton, George, *On the Eightfold Path: Christian Presence Amid Buddhism.* New York: Oxford University Press, 1961.

Cragg, Kenneth, *Sandals at the Mosque: Christian Presence Amid Islam.* New York: Oxford University Press, 1959.

Hammer, Raymond, *Japan's Religious Ferment: Christian Presence Amid Faiths Old and New.* New York: Oxford University Press, 1962.

Latourette, Kenneth Scott, *Introducing Buddhism.* New York: Friendship Press, 1956.

Nida, Eugene A. and William A. Smalley, *Introducing Animism.* New York: Friendship Press, 1959.

Pitt, Malcolm, *Introducing Hinduism.* New York: Friendship Press, 1955.

Taylor, John V., *The Primal Vision: Christian Presence Amid African Religion.* Philadelphia: Fortress Press, 1964.

Wilson, J. Christy, *Introducing Islam.* New York: Friendship Press, 1958.

COMPARATIVE RELIGIONS

Bouquet, A. C., *Sacred Books of the World* (anthology with commentary). New York: Barnes and Noble, 1962.

Jackson, Herbert C., *Man Reaches Out to God: Living Religions and the Christian Missionary Obligation.* Valley Forge, Pa.: Judson Press, 1963.

Kitagawa, Joseph M., *Religions of the East.* Philadelphia: Westminster Press, 1960.

Parrinder, Geoffrey, *Worship in the World's Religions.* London: Faber and Faber, 1961.

Pike, E. Ralston (ed.), *Encyclopedia of Religion and Religions.* Cleveland: The World Publishing Co., 1958.

Smith, Huston, *The Religions of Man.* New York: Harper and Row, 1958.

Stowe, David M., *When Faith Meets Faith.* New York: Friendship Press, 1967 (rev. ed.).

FAITH AND RELIGION

Anderson, Gerald H., *Sermons to Men of Other Faiths and Traditions.* Nashville: Abingdon Press, 1966.

Cooke, Gerald, *As Christians Face Rival Religions: An Interreligious Strategy for Community Without Compromise.* New York: Association Press, 1962.

Ferré, Nels F. S., *The Finality of Faith.* New York: Harper and Row, 1963.

Gundry, D. W., *Religions: A Preliminary Historical and Theological Study.* London: Macmillan, 1958.

Perry, Edmund F., *The Gospel in Dispute: The Relation of Christian Faith to Other Religions.* Garden City, N.Y.: Doubleday, 1958.

Smith, Wilfred Cantwell, *The Meaning and End of Religion.* New York: Macmillan, 1962.

Tillich, Paul, *Dynamics of Faith.* New York: Harper and Row, 1957.

FAITH, RELIGION AND CONTEMPORARY CRISIS

Butterfield, Herbert, *Christianity and History.* New York: Scribner, 1950.

————, *International Conflict in the Twentieth Century: A Christian View.* New York: Harper and Row, 1960.

Considine, John J. (ed.), *Social Revolution in the New Latin America.* Notre Dame, Indiana: Fides Publishers, 1965.

Dodds, Elizabeth D. (compiler), *Voices of Protest and Hope* (an anthology). New York: Friendship Press, 1965.

Evans, Donald, *Communist Faith and Christian Faith.* London: SCM Press, 1965.

Dawson, Christopher, *The Historic Reality of Christian Culture.* New York: Harper and Row, 1960.

Muller, Herbert J., *Religion and Freedom in the Modern World.* Chicago: University of Chicago Press, 1963.

Niebuhr, Reinhold, *The Children of Light and the Children of Darkness.* New York: Scribner, 1960.

Webber, George W., *God's Colony in Man's World.* Nashville: Abingdon Press, 1960.

Williams, Colin, *For the World.* New York: National Council of Churches, 1965.

# 174 · ENCOUNTER OF THE FAITHS

PREPARATION FOR DIALOGUE

Althouse, Lavonne, *When Jew and Christian Meet.* New York: Friendship Press, 1966.

Greenspun, William B. and William A. Norgren (eds.), *Living Room Dialogues.* New York: NCC, or Glen Rock, N.J.: Paulist Press, 1966.

Neill, Stephen, *Christian Faith and Other Faiths: The Christian Dialogue with Other Religions.* New York: Oxford University Press, 1961.

## ABOUT THE FORMAT

The text of this book is set in Caledonia, 10 point leaded
3 points. Designed by the late W. A. Dwiggins, this lino-
type face belongs to the "modern" family of type
faces and is somewhat similar to Scotch
Modern, although more freely
drawn than that letter.

Typographic design by Margery W. Smith